MANAGING SPECIAL NEEDS IN MAINSTREAM SCHOOLS

The Role of the SENCO

Edited by

John Dwyfor Davies, Philip Garner and John Lee

David Fulton Publishers

London

London WC1N 3JD

d Fulton Publishers 1998

Note: The right of John Dwyfor Davies, Philip Garner and John Lee to be identified as the authors of this work has been asserted by them in accordance with the Copyright, Designs and Patents Act 1988.

British Library Cataloguing in Publication Data
A catalogue record for this book is available from the British Library

ISBN 1–85346–526–7

Typeset by FSH Ltd, London
Printed in Great Britain by BPC Books and Journals, Exeter

Contents

Contributors

Kathy Bale is SENCO at Trafalgar Junior School, Twickenham.

Hazel Bines is Professor and Assistant Dean in the Faculty of Health, Social Work and Education at the University of Northumbria.

Gillian Blunden is Director of Research at the Faculty of Health and Social Care, University of the West of England, Bristol. She is also the governor with responsibility for special educational needs at a maintained infant school.

John Cornwall is a senior lecturer in the Special Needs Research and Development Centre, Christchurch College, Canterbury.

John Dwyfor Davies is Principal Lecturer and Director of Studies (CPD) in the Faculty of Education, University of the West of England, Bristol.

Jim Docking is a Researcher at Roehampton Institute, London.

Tony Duckett is Learning Support Coordinator, Queensmead School, Ruislip, Middlesex.

Roy Evans is Research Fellow in the Centre for Comparative Studies in Special Education at Brunel University.

William Evans is a solicitor and was formerly secretary and solicitor to the University of the West of England, Bristol.

Philip Garner is Reader in Education in the School of Education, Brunel University.

Stephen Grant is the Vice Chair of Bristol Council's Education Committee and also serves on its Social Services Committee. He is Chair of Governors of a maintained secondary school and a newly amalgamated primary school.

Lesley Kaplan is a district senior educational psychologist in Bristol.

John Lee is Principal Lecturer in Education at the Faculty of Education, University of the West of England, Bristol.

Veronica Lee is the head teacher of a small primary school in the West Country.

Sue Rice is the deputy head teacher of a nursery school in the West Country.

Peter Russell is SENCO in a middle school in East Anglia.

Sheila Russell is SENCO in a first school in East Anglia.

Alison Scott-Baumann is an educational psychologist in Bristol and also Senior Lecturer at Cheltenham and Gloucester College of Higher Education.

Jane Tarr is Senior Lecturer in Education at the Faculty of Education, University of the West of England, Bristol.

Gary Thomas is Professor of Education in the Faculty of Education, University of the West of England, Bristol.

Janet Tod is Principal Lecturer and Head of the Special Needs Research and Development Centre, Christchurch College, Canterbury.

Abbreviations

ADHD	Attention Deficit & Hyperactivity Disorder
ASB	Aggregated School Budget
AWPU	Age Weighted Pupil Unit
CoP	Code of Practice
CPD	Continuing Professional Development
DfE	Department for Education
DfEE	Department for Education and Employment
EBD	Emotional and/or Behahavioural Difficulties
EP	Educational Psychologist
EPS	Educational Psychology Service
EWO	Education Welfare Worker
GEST	Grants for Education Support and Training
GSB	General School Budget
HMI	Her Majesty's Inspectorate
IEP	Individual Education Plan
IHE	Institution of Higher Education
INSET	In-service Education and Training
LEA	Local Education Authority
LMS	Local Management of Schools
LSA	Learning Support Assistant
MLD	Moderate Learning Difficulties
KS	Key Stage
MA	Master of Arts
MDA	Mid-day Supervisory Assistant
MEd	Masters in Education
NCC	National Curriculum Council
NNEB	National Nurses Education Board
OFSTED	Office for Standards in Education
PANDAS	Performance and Assessment
PSHE	Personal, Social and Health Education

PTA   Parent Teacher Association
RSA   Royal Society of Arts
SAT   Standard Assessment Tests
SDP   School Development Plan
SEAT   Special Education Advisory Team
SENCO   Special Educational Needs Coordinator
SENSC   Special Educational Needs Support Centre
SENTC   Special Educational Needs Training Consortium
SLD   Severe Learning Difficulties
SMT   Senior Management Team

Introduction

Sarah Bowman is viewed by her colleagues at St Vincent's Primary School as a pivotal figure in school organisation. She is frequently called upon to provide guidance and support to teachers in the school, whilst at the same time managing a class of her own. The period before school, during morning break and at lunch-time are her favoured times for the practice of what she refers to as 'collaring' those she works with to discuss SEN matters.

At other times, frequently in the evenings and weekends, Sarah's time is taken up with maintaining the school's documentation for the staged assessment under the Code of Practice and planning and monitoring IEPs. She has a full meeting schedule, comprising senior management team meetings, review meetings, meetings with parents, meetings with collaborating professionals, and what she refers to as a 'normal' diet of assessment meetings, curriculum discussions and other gatherings.

Sarah's wide-ranging role and its commensurate heavy workload will be familiar to those primary school teachers who occupy the post of Special Educational Needs Coordinator (SENCO). Hers is a fairly typical story, which confirms the paradoxical impact of the creation of the role following the Education Act, 1993. What has subsequently become apparent is that the status of a new breed of teachers, the SENCO, has been significantly enhanced.

Such are the wide-ranging responsibilities of SENCOs in the 1990s that they seem light years away from the frequently marginalised role that 'remedial' teachers held just 30 or so years previously. There is an increased level of responsibility and status which Sarah gladly accepted when she was offered the post of SENCO at St Vincent's in 1996. Her belief was that 'I would have been foolish not to accept it. Of course I knew that there would be a lot of extra work, but I realised that the position was really influential. I could do something to change things because I had the power.'

At the same time, however, this enhanced position of the newly established role of SENCO within the decision-making machinery of primary schools was accompanied by a level of responsibility and an increase in workload which have become salient features of the professional culture of the post. It is unlikely that those who first assumed the role were fully aware of the extent to which their job would become so time-consuming and, at times, frustrating.

So, whilst Sarah recognised the potential for an increase in her workload, she admits that there are times when she feels overwhelmed: 'I can take the pressure of the responsibility that being a SENCO involves, but I sometimes panic when I realise how many people depend on the bits of paper I have to process.'

Both perspectives do much to articulate the concerns of SENCOs in general. Concomitant to this situation is that the SENCO has a statutory requirement to fulfil certain duties and this has legal ramifications, as William Evans points out in this book and as is now becoming evident as individual parents litigate against local educational authorities (LEAs) or individual schools. Little attention was initially given to the degree to which the persons appointed as SENCOs were familiar with the legislation underpinning the role (notably the 1993 Education Act and the 1994 Code of Practice). Some held no additional qualifications in SEN and others had received little associated training or professional development relating to SEN. In consequence, there was ample evidence to support the anxiety felt by SENCOs, in the period immediately following the implementation of the Code, regarding their ability to fulfil their new role effectively. And whilst LEAs, often in partnership with Institutions of Higher Education (IHEs) were quick to provide training courses for SENCOs, such experiences may not have been tailored to meet the needs of SENCOs in a wide variety of primary schools; the Code and the role of SENCO were a new departure for all concerned, not least for the trainers themselves! Subsequently, of course, the skills, knowledge and attributes needed to undertake the role of SENCO successfully have become the subject of much discussion and reflection. The Special Educational Needs Training Consortium (SENTC) has been active hereabouts (SENTC 1996) and the TTA has published its proposals for programmes of study specifically designed to delineate the numerous elements of the SENCO role.

Excellent though these initiatives may be, we need to remind ourselves that, in the majority of primary schools, teachers are not simply responsible for pupils with special educational needs, but, like Sarah Bowman, teach a class and often manage at least one other curriculum area. Hazel Bines, in her contribution to this book, has quite rightly, if somewhat reservedly, described this as 'an extremely demanding agenda'. The content of this book represents the thinking, on the part of SENCOs themselves and a range of other professionals, on what it is to be a SENCO in a primary school at the present time. The role has now become culturally embedded in the practices of the primary school, and is approaching some kind of maturity. Individual schools, and the SENCOs within them, have discharged their responsibilities differently. Thus, whilst the statutory requirements of the Code of Practice have largely been accommodated, the way in which SENCOs choose to operate has varied according to the requirements and capabilities of individual schools, thus amplifying the 'guidance' of the Code that it should be seen as a flexible set of recommendations which can (and should) be adapted according to the needs of individual contexts.

In this book several SENCOs discuss the manner in which they have adapted the role to meet the needs of children, their school and, perhaps most important, their own vision of special needs provision. Peter and Sheila Russell, for instance, show how they make the 'system' work for individual pupils and, in doing so, argue for a particular educational orientation. Kathy Bale uses the bureaucratic nature of the role in a very different way from Sue Rice, who is somewhat sceptical of IEPs and all that comes with them. And Veronica Lee describes how a small school not merely copes but enhances the educational experience of very special pupils.

One aspect of the SENCO's duties which has come under considerable scrutiny is, as the role-title makes explicit, its coordinating function. The SENCO, for example, is in a unique position in linking individual pupils to resources and support agencies, both within and outside the school. Tony Duckett reminds us that there is a particular role that the primary SENCO plays in communicating with colleagues in secondary schools at the point of transfer, whilst communicating something of the excitement of the move for individual pupils. The maturation of the role of SENCO has been paralleled by the refined relationships which now frequently exist with educational psychologists (EP). This link has often been a delicate one, with teachers viewing the EP (in many cases wrongly) as being too removed from the reality of the classroom and as gate-keepers to further resources. Too often this resulted in conflict between the two parties. The chapter by Alison Scott-Baumann and Lesley Kaplan describes one approach that has been successfully implemented, incorporating the kind of collaborative approach which is becoming more indicative of 'second generation' SENCO practice.

Although William Evans has noted that the role of SENCO is potentially a legal minefield, it should be emphasised that it is the governing body of a school that is ultimately responsible for SEN provision. It has, therefore, become increasingly apparent that primary school teachers have to establish an effective working relationship with their governing body. For instance, the language coordinator will, in future, have to form a close and special relationship with the literacy governor. In many schools SENCOs already provide a role model for the establishment of such a relationship. It is a requirement that all schools identify a named governor responsible for monitoring and ensuring that the school's SEN policy is actively followed and that appropriate provision is in place to meet the needs of pupils with learning difficulties. Gillian Blunden and Stephen Grant discuss this potentially thorny issue.

At the time of writing, the teachers' associations are urging the government to reduce the paper work required of teachers. They argue, and the government agrees, that it is better to spend less time on paperwork and more time planning and teaching lessons. Admirable though such sentiments are, it remains difficult to see how the paper workload of the SENCO can be radically reduced. Jane Tarr and Gary Thomas point to the challenge of writing SEN policies and the crucial role of the SENCO in that. Janet Tod and John Cornwall, as well as Kathy Bale, remind us that Individual Education Plans (IEPs) do not come ready made, but are the result of many hours of careful work. It is easy to take the view that the role of SENCO in primary schools is fraught with difficulty, heavy workload and the spectre of litigation. Each of these is an important concern and they have featured repeatedly in SENCO discussion and debate, and in the initial research studies on the role, in the period immediately following the implementation of the Code. Nor would we want to underestimate the volume of work and the pressures involved – both personal and professional – in being a SENCO.

Since 1988, LEAs have had to function in a new and challenging context. In many ways, the introduction of the Code of Practice was the first real test of the new relationship which had evolved between schools and the LEAs. Prior to 1988, the LEA was the fulcrum for coordinating inter-agency work, but this has since been largely devolved to individual SENCOs and has consequently become one of the key features of that role. Roy Evans and Jim Docking, in their chapter, examine in some detail this new relationship between SENCOs and the LEA.

The views of the contributors to this volume are, perhaps, indicative of the evolving and maturing nature of the post. They demonstrate that, in accepting a challenging role, SENCOs find a way through. They solve problems in a variety of imaginative ways which crucially reflect the context within which they work. If the remaining years leading to the millennium result in a similar level of innovation and commitment, it seems likely that the position occupied by SENCOs at the heart of provision for those with learning difficulty will be confirmed and enhanced.

Chapter 1

Operating in the context of zero tolerance

John Dwyfor Davies, Philip Garner and John Lee

The passing of the 1988 Education Reform Act Act marked the beginning of a period of remarkable volatility in English and Welsh education policy. Since that time, the system has been subject to an extraordinary range of centrally generated policy initiatives. All schools and teachers have been subject to this 'bearing down' of the central state, but it will be argued that this pressure is especially severe on SENCOs. In parallel with legislation and administrative orders, we have seen the development of fierce ideological debates around the concepts of integration and inclusion, with their accompanying rhetoric. The purpose of this chapter is to place the SENCO's role and operation in the context of broad policy and administrative changes since the General Election of 1997.

The change of government in 1997 has brought about a flurry of new policies and legislation. Elected on the slogan 'education, education, education', it has declared itself to be committed to raising standards for all pupils in all schools. It has produced two major education green papers, a white paper, and currently two bills are progressing through parliament.[1] The general welcome given to the change of government by the teachers' professional associations and their old 'partners' the LEAs, was to some extent predicated on the notion that the new government would be less interventionist, and more trusting of the profession. This has proved to be ill-founded. This government, rather than 'getting off teachers' backs', has been equally, if not more, aggressive than the previous in directing what teachers must do and how schools should be organised. Some of these policies and the institutions that are related to them are a continuation from the previous government, others are new. We identify the following as impacting in particular ways on the role of the SENCO.

- OFSTED inspection and Performance and Assessment reports (PANDAs)
- The development of national, local and school-based achievement targets for literacy and numeracy
- The National Literacy Strategy
- The National Numeracy Strategy
- Moves towards a reduction in Stage 4/5 statements
- Moves towards increased integration/inclusivity.

Inspection, School Evaluation and Performance

While it is true that the process and results of inspection are significant in the life of all teachers, and there is a good deal of evidence that inspection causes stress for teachers (see for instance Duffy n.d., Jeffrey and Woods 1996), the impact of both inspection procedures on SENCOs is considerable, and this will undoubtedly increase as schools are expected to meet targets for literacy and numeracy. The most recent annual inspection report recognises the role of SENCOs in making appropriate provision for pupils with special educational needs.

> Provision for pupils with special educational needs is good in six in ten schools and rarely inadequate. The Code of Practice has helped schools to improve the match of the provision to the needs of pupils. Special needs coordinators have established appropriate procedures for keeping a register of pupils' special educational needs and for preparing and revising individual action plans. However, many coordinators are concerned about the time taken for this and have been unable to complete the recommended termly reviews. (OFSTED 1998a)

At present SENCOs are heavily involved in the preparation of documentation before inspection. More significantly, they can be called to account for the procedures followed in schools for the identification of pupils with special educational needs, the monitoring of their progress and the advice they give to colleagues with respect to these pupils. It is true that all subject coordinators in primary schools are accountable to OFSTED, but the situation for SENCOs is rather different. Unlike their colleagues, SENCOs have a responsibility for ensuring that the Code of Practice has been followed and that adequate documentation has been kept. Further, SENCOs must be able to account for the reviewing of pupils' progress once they are on the special needs register, yet there appears to be little time for this. None of this is the result of policy changes initiated by the Labour government. But the focus on the setting of absolute standards and the government's confidence in the use of inspection in achieving that policy goal puts SENCOs in this difficult and stressful position.

The recent publication *School Evaluation Matters* (OFSTED 1998b) advises schools that in addition to external evaluation – inspection – they ought to engage in self-evaluation. The tone of the document chimes with the relentless policy demands of the government for school improvement. It states:

> You should therefore base any strategy for improvement on systematic monitoring of performance and evaluation of classroom practice to provide *a clear diagnosis of how teaching and learning can be more effective* (emphasis ours).

The role of the SENCO in this will be crucial for children who are on the register. SENCOs must monitor and advise on the teaching methods to be adopted for pupils with special educational needs. The progress of pupils with IEPs will be under scrutiny with respect not just to individual progress but to the effectivity of the school. The Chief Inspector's *Annual Report* (1998a) identifies the lack of time to complete pupil reviews as a problem. More problematic will be the fact that SENCOs will be addressing the question of how schools can become more effective with respect to pupils with special educational needs, in a context in which 'monitoring, evaluation and support for teaching' was judged to be unsatisfactory in 62 per cent of primary schools in 1996/97 (OFSTED 1997).

As schools begin to use Performance and Assessment reports, it is very likely that SENCOs will be expected to help to identify similar schools. The number of pupils with special educational needs is significant in any form of benchmarking, and it is likely that SENCOs will be 'pushed' to generate more Stage 3 statements, particularly in those schools that compare unfavourably in terms of performance with others in their locality.

National, local and school targets

The Labour government came to power on manifesto promises to prioritise education. It has accepted the view of the previous administration that schools provide poor-quality education for too many pupils. Before the election of May 1997, the Labour party declared that it was its intention to ensure that standards in literacy and numeracy were raised in all schools. Once elected, it declared absolute standards to be met in these core skills. On 13 May 1997, David Blunkett, Secretary of State for Education, announced these new standards.

> Last year, in national tests only 55% of our 11 year olds finishing their crucial primary school years reached the standards in maths expected for their age. In English tests only 57% could read at the same standard. These are weaknesses in absolutely basic skills at vital moments in the lives of our children – and we must tackle them. That's why today I am announcing that by the time of the national tests in 2002: 75% of 11 year olds will be reaching the standards expected for their age in maths, and 80% of 11 year olds will be reaching the standards expected for their age in English. (DfEE 1997c)

These absolute standards are defined as Level 4 in English and mathematics at the end of Key Stage 2, and must be reached regardless of the pupils' social backgrounds. In January 1998 Steven Byers, School Standards Minister, set out how the targets were to be delivered. Each LEA has now been set an individual target.

> These figures have been agreed with LEAs and they are tough. For example: in Sandwell LEA in 1996, 45% of 11 year olds reached the standard required for their age in English tests by 2002 it must be 76%; in Tower Hamlets the 1996 figure was 36%, by 2002 it must be 70%...others are currently above the national average but there is no room for complacency. For example: in Bromley, the 1996 figure was 67%, in 2002 it must be 90%; in Bury, the 1996 figure was 66%, in 2002 it must be 90%.... We want no excuses for failure. Many LEAs are in deprived areas, but poverty is no excuse for underachievement. (DfEE 1998a)

This policy does not set out aspirations but is a series of imperatives. LEAs must reach these standards regardless of their individual circumstances. Whilst social disadvantage is recognised, it is barely taken into account in setting the targets. Having received their targets, LEAs have now given targets to each of their schools. While the national targets apparently recognise Warnock's contention that 20 per cent of the school population will have special educational needs at any given time, this percentage will not be evident in every school. Such is the very harsh climate in which SENCOs must operate. SENCOs will be placed in the position of advocating specific provision for pupils with special educational needs, in institutions with fixed achievement targets. Most SENCOs hold the view that the recognition of individual differences and achievements of individuals, however small, is the way to meet the needs of particular pupils. Although charged with responsibility for pupils, they have no role in setting achievement targets for them and may well find themselves in conflict with national, local and school policy directives.

There is already some anecdotal evidence of schools rejecting pupils who they think may adversely affect their KS1 and 2 assessment averages, because they have either learning difficulties or behavioural difficulties. SENCOs are likely to be placed in a position of being the advocate for such children, putting themselves in professional – and possibly personal – conflict with their colleagues.

Turning to Individual Education Plans (IEPs), there is a problem here in that the IEP must relate directly to the identified needs of the child. For instance, it may set a slower pace of learning for individuals. Equally, while ensuring the pupil's entitlement to the National Curriculum, the IEP will necessarily prioritise some skills and knowledge above others. This will inevitably lead to conflict with the school's prioritisation of meeting its set literacy and numeracy targets. We suggest that this will arise at two levels. First, the slight freedom of action that is currently enjoyed in meeting the demands of pupils with special educational needs will be constrained as resources are mobilised to meet the school's target demands. Second, the change in pedagogy that will be brought about by the focus on literacy and numeracy will remove the capacity of individual class teachers to plan for individuals. In both these cases, the arguments that the SENCOs make for provision may place them in conflict with both their colleagues and their managers.

National strategies

The 1988 Education Act directed schools as to the content of the curriculum but maintained the long tradition of allowing teachers and schools to teach in the way they felt to be most appropriate. Also explicitly excluded from legislation was the amount of time to be spent on different subjects. During the second reading of the bill, the Secretary of State, Kenneth Baker, in his speech to the House of Commons, made these points abundantly clear.

> We do not intend to lay down, either on the face of the Bill or in any secondary legislation, the percentage of time to be spent on different subjects. This will provide flexibility, but it is our belief that it will be difficult, if not impossible, for any school to provide the national curriculum in less than 70% of the time available... We want to build on the professionalism of the many fine teachers and dedicated teachers throughout our education system. The national curriculum will provide scope for imaginative approaches developed by our teachers. (Haviland 1988)

It is worth reminding ourselves that when Kenneth Baker made this speech in December 1987, he was speaking in support of what was deemed to be the most centralising piece of education legislation ever. Reading this speech now, it is evident how amazingly bold and innovative the Labour government has been with respect to pedagogy. The national strategies for literacy and numeracy prescribe content, time allocation per subject and teaching method. The national targets for literacy and numeracy, discussed above, will be met because schools and teachers will follow the specified pedagogy. At the time of writing only the *National Literacy Strategy Framework for Teaching* (DfEE 1998a) has been published. The *National Numeracy Strategy* (DfEE 1998b) is still in draft form published for consultation. But its time allocations and teaching procedures mirror that of the Literacy Strategy. Thus we can be confident in stating that its effects will be similar. It is to the nature of this pedagogy and its origins that we now turn.

The pedagogy of the two strategies is claimed to be firmly underpinned by research findings. In fact, it draws very heavily on the school effectiveness literature. Mortimore *et al.* (1988) study of ILEA junior schools is the source of many of the ideas underpinning the strategies. They found that the effective classrooms observed were characterised by regular, high order cognitive interactions and a correspondingly lower number of managerial and organisational ones. It was not simply a matter of teachers prioritising cognitive interactions that was significant, but that they interacted regularly with all the children in the class. Later, classroom effectiveness studies have also pointed to this as an important correlate of classroom effectiveness. What we would point to as important here is the fact that it is the actions of teachers as instructors, rather than as organisers and facilitators, that is the measure of effectiveness.

The two strategies can be seen as the practical working out of the broad policy objective of refusing to tolerate failure – 'zero tolerance'. As well as the school effectiveness research, it draws on the idea that schools cannot/should not be allowed to fail, what is often referred to as 'high reliability'. This aspect of school effectiveness prioritises specified outcomes for all, and plays down the idea that the make-up of the school population should be taken into account.

At a conference on 27 February 1997, approximately three months before the election of the Labour party, the introduction of a literacy 'task force' was announced. In fact, what the task force presented as a vision has become reality. An important aspect of the conference was the way in which the overarching idea of no tolerance for failure was highlighted and Slavin's 'Success for All' project (Slavin 1997) was presented as a key case study. In fact, Slavin himself addressed the conference. His was an optimistic and upbeat contribution, assuring the conference that it was possible to ensure that schools delivered success to their pupils – even if those pupils were amongst the poverty-stricken and disadvantaged. The claims for 'Success for All' programmes are impressive. Slavin argues that 'large scale change in teaching practices can be brought about through the development, evaluation, and dissemination of proven, replicable programs.' His vignette of a school day presented teachers following a prescribed set of teaching procedures in given time slots. But the requirements of the programme segment the day, not the needs of individual children or the individual plans of their teachers.

What we can see in the National Literacy Strategy (DfEE 1998a), and its accompanying hour, is a prescribed programme similar to that argued for by Slavin. It is worth considering in some detail what the structure of the Literacy Hour is.

Table 1.1 Structure of the Literacy Hour

15 minutes	15 minutes	20 minutes	10 minutes
Whole-class shared text	Whole-class word and sentence work	Group and independent work	Whole-class review and consolidation
Undifferentiated	Undifferentiated	Differentiated	Undifferentiated

Drawing on the idea that at least 80 per cent of children should progress to meet set targets, 40 minutes of the hour are given over to work which is not differentiated for individual needs.

Table 1.2 Content of the Literacy Hour

Content of the hour		
Word level	**Sentence level**	**Text level**
Reception year		
Phonological awareness	Grammatical awareness	Understanding of print
Phonics and spelling		Reading comprehension
Vocabulary extension		Writing composition
Handwriting		
Key Stage 1		
Phonological awareness	Grammatical awareness	*Fiction and poetry*
Phonics and spelling	Sentence construction and	Reading comprehension
Word recognition, graphic	punctuation	Writing composition
knowledge and spelling		*Non-fiction*
Vocabulary extension		Reading and comprehension
Handwriting		Writing composition

Key Stage 2		
Revision and consolidation from Key Stage 1 (to the end of Year 3)	Grammatical awareness	*Fiction and poetry*
	Sentence construction and punctuation	Reading comprehension
Spelling strategies		Writing composition
Spelling conventions and rules		*Non-fiction*
		Reading comprehension
Vocabulary extension		Writing composition
Handwriting (to the end of Year 4)		

This general content is spelt out in termly detail for reception children and for Key Stages 1 and 2. Even a cursory consideration of the content indicates problems for SENCOs. The content objectives set out above presume that pupils will achieve knowledge, understanding and skills specified for Key Stage 1 by the end of Year 3 at the latest.

We noted that the content specified by the framework is undifferentiated. The draft proposal for the numeracy framework offers the same undifferentiated content. It is not simply the content but also the pedagogy that will impact on SENCOs. The focus of the general policy is pedagogical, a belief that only by following the pedagogical prescriptions of the two hours will 'success for all' come about. The nature of the Code of Practice and the sorts of practices and actions it has engendered have focused attention on individual needs and differentiated provision. SENCOs both expect and are expected to make pedagogical suggestions and to revise content to meet the needs of individuals. This runs counter to the relentless insistence that content and pedagogy must be common. Although the Literacy and Numeracy Hours are not compulsory, not framed in legislation as is the National Curriculum, they have the feel of compulsion:

> While the Framework provides details of what should be taught, the Literacy Hour is the means of teaching it. The Literacy Hour should be implemented throughout the school to provide a daily period of dedicated literacy time for all pupils. (DfEE, 1998a)

Differentiation has been a key concept for SENCOs. It has been argued that work must be differentiated to meet the needs of pupils and that pupils with special educational needs are the paradigm case for the practice. It is difficult to see how the introduction of these new pedagogies will not bring with them professional and perhaps personal conflict for SENCOs.

It has been common practice in many schools to provide small group and/or one-to-one teaching for pupils with special educational needs. A recent OFSTED report praised a primary school for precisely such an arrangement, commenting very favourably on its benefits to pupils with special educational needs and others. The reduction in flexibility with regard to the class and school timetable will challenge these practices. The advent of the National Curriculum made withdrawal for the teaching of reading and remedial work in number problematic. However, this has been overcome to some extent by pupils being taught in small groups as opposed to the whole class. Even so, there is some anecdotal evidence that pupils with special educational needs have a reduced curriculum in schools where small-group withdrawal is a practice.

The future for such arrangements appears problematic. It is unlikely that the practice can survive once both Literacy and Numeracy Hours are in place. However, classroom teachers will still have the expectation that SENCOs will make arrangements for the teaching of pupils with special educational needs. The use of small-group methods, both within the classroom and outside, addresses the needs of the pupils and the needs of the class teachers. SENCOs will be faced with the problem of 'educating' their colleagues in new forms of support for pupils. They will have to convince their colleagues that use of resources within classrooms as part of the Hours is not a diminution in resourcing, and that it is not merely more efficient but also more effective.

An important aspect of the pedagogical organisation of both the Hours is a focus on teacher–pupil verbal interaction.

The most successful teaching is:

- discursive – characterised by high quality oral work;
- interactive – pupils' contributions are encouraged, expected and extended;
- well-paced – there is sense of urgency, driven by the need to make progress and succeed. (DfEE 1998a)

The organisation of the Hours places great emphasis on whole-class teaching. In the case of the Literacy Hour, for instance, each lesson begins with 30 minutes during which the children sit on the carpet and are expected to respond to the teacher's questions. The requirement to sit, listen and respond is very challenging for a number of pupils. Many SENCOs take the role of being the advocate for pupils with challenging behaviour, explaining to their colleagues how they can ameliorate circumstances so that these pupils can cope and be coped with. The problem for the SENCOs is likely to be the conflict that arises from the rigidity of the pedagogical organisation and their instincts to advise colleagues to deal with pupils with behavioural difficulties in specific and special ways.

Problems with the early acquisition of reading are regularly taken as indicative of pupils who have special educational needs (Croll and Moses 1985) and such pupils have traditionally become the responsibility of SENCOs. The introduction of the Literacy Hour brings with it an extended role for English coordinators in primary schools. The potential for role conflict over who manages the teaching and learning for pupils deemed to be failing readers is high. It is not our intention here to create professional rivalries and jealousies where they do not exist. It would be foolish to assume that in some circumstances they will not appear. At moments of institutional stress such as OFSTED inspection and its consequences such personal/professional problems may well occur.

Moves towards inclusion

Since the publication of the Warnock Report (DES 1978), there has been a continuing drive to reduce the number of pupils educated in special schools. Croll and Moses (1998) comment on the decline in the number of special schools since 1982 and suggest that this 'reflects contemporary judgements about the sorts of provision which are appropriate'. What has happened over these years has been the integration/inclusion of pupils into mainstream schools, with an emphasis in the first instance on those with mild learning difficulties. More recently, we have seen the development of an ideological debate over the school placement of pupils with special educational needs. Those arguing the case for inclusive education have seized the moral high ground, taking an explicit ideological position and arguing from convictions about social justice and equality of provision. Because of the nature of their roles and responsibilities SENCOs are caught within the web of this debate.

The general move to include pupils with special educational needs in the mainstream is at least in part a tribute to the work of SENCOs. As noted above, they have been powerful advocates. In addition, they have been seen as the source of specialist knowledge which can be drawn upon by class teachers. Over the years, they have also developed an expertise in liaising with external services in both the assessment of pupils' needs and the writing of IEPs and analogous action plans. However, if the debate over inclusion becomes more strident, SENCOs may be positioned by colleagues as proponents of a policy which they see as extremely problematic. The recent claims by teacher associations that pupils with Emotional and Behavioural Difficulties (EBD) are becoming a serious problem for classroom teachers will put SENCOs in the situation we allude to above.

And another thing

We have sketched out some of the challenges that SENCOs now face and are likely to face in the future, as a result of current government policy. However, these are not the only policy changes that will affect SENCOs directly. The creation of Education Action Zones will place SENCOs in an interesting position with respect to the improvement of education for all disadvantaged pupils in these new organisations. It is proposed that 'expert professionals' will be recruited, class teachers who will demonstrate the highest level of professional skill. These will presumably, in part, be judged on their ability to deal with pupils with special educational needs. Since they will be expected to advise their colleagues, it is unclear how this aspect of their role will be differentiated from that of the SENCO. In the end, it is the inexorable push of two related policies – first, the demand that the majority of pupils reach exactly the same standards, and, second, a requirement that these standards be delivered using similar pedagogies – that will cause most concern for SENCOs.

Notes

1 At the time of writing (March 1998) both the Teaching and Higher Education Bill and the School Standards Framework Bill are in their third reading and are expected to receive royal assent in the life of this parliament.

Chapter 2

An extremely demanding agenda

Hazel Bines

Whatever reservations might be felt about particular directions and details of policies and legislation, at least the SENCO, and the management of special educational needs (SEN) in mainstream schools, are now visible in national policy making and debate. This marks considerable progress from the days when curriculum development initiatives, ranging from Schools' Council projects through TVEI to the implementation of a National Curriculum, tended to see SEN as an afterthought, and from times when the management of SEN was narrowly perceived in terms of small amounts of remedial teaching provision. Those involved in SEN work in schools, together with organisations such as the National Association for Special Educational Needs, have finally managed to generate interest, debate and intervention at both local and national levels, so that the effective management of SEN is now seen as a crucial element of schools in general.

However, this public spotlight is beginning to have some disadvantages. As other authors in this volume explore, there is now a huge range of expectations and pressures on the SENCO and an extremely demanding agenda to fulfil. This chapter will trace some of the most significant aspects of that agenda. It will also consider some of the gaps in national policy making which continue to exist, and predict some probable policy themes for the future. The basis of the chapter will be that although the focus on SENCO work will inevitably be a particular school, it is important to reflect on the way such work fits into broader trends and contexts and how that wider framework can be interpreted to aid more effective work at local levels.

Education policy has been the subject of a lot of research and analytical interest in recent years, particularly since the implementation of the Education Reform Act in 1988. The radical nature of some of the changes involved in that Act has resulted in a shift in policy studies from administrative and organisational aspects of policy towards the key political and policy themes involved in particular reforms, how these have been conceptualised and expressed, and how subsequent policy changes are then implemented by the participants involved. Emphasis has also been laid on links between different aspects of policy, within and across particular public and other services. Although such analysis has not been widely applied by those working in the SEN field, and SEN issues have sometimes been neglected by education policy analysts themselves, it is possible to draw on such approaches in relation to the management of SEN in schools. In particular we can learn from some of the weaknesses of some education policy analysis to date, namely the lack of an historical or temporal dimension, and the tendency to see policy development and implementation as a tidy and linear process, instead of a somewhat messy mix of negotiation, conflict and change which above all involves people, many of whom will have very different beliefs, experiences and interests. This chapter will therefore take this more open approach, focusing on particularly significant policy themes and texts.

The recent period of policy making on SEN

Recent changes in government, and in certain government policies, make this a difficult time to reflect on either the past or the future, particularly given the approach of a new millennium which promises even more rapid social and other change. Nevertheless, it is possible to identify the last 20 years or so as a particular and significant period of policy making in relation to SEN, starting with the Warnock Report and 1981 Education Act and finishing with the recent Code of Practice.

The 1981 Act, and related Warnock Report, are a crucial starting point because of the more flexible and wider-ranging definition of special educational needs which they introduced. This continues to be the definition on which subsequent policies, such as the Code of Practice, have been based. They also laid the basis for a differentiated and staged approach, based on severity of need and/or degree of specialised provision required, which has also continued to shape policy. In addition, the more explicit commitment to integration as a policy intention reflected in the 1981 Act provided an important impetus for future policy making. Recognition of the extent of learning and other difficulties in mainstream schools also legitimated the moving of what were then called remedial education and remedial teachers from a marginal position into more central and integrated roles focusing on support to enable pupils to access the curriculum more effectively (Bines 1986).

At the same time such changes had their roots in the 1944 Education Act, and can be seen as the final completion of the universalist agenda of ensuring equal access to education for all children as originally promised by that Act (Welton 1988). Policy in this period therefore drew upon a conception of educational entitlement as being primarily an issue of access. And although definitions of need became more flexible, they continued to incorporate traditional notions of educability enshrined in the 1944 Education Act, namely that learning and other difficulties are rooted in pupils rather than the education system, and that different forms of provision, rather than fundamental changes in mainstream schooling, are therefore required. Although it was the intention to reduce categorisation, and replace it with notions of a continuum, the labelling of particular needs remained, which, when set alongside stages of 'specialness', created a potential matrix for various procedures and interventions based on deficits and being different. The approach to the policy process was also rooted in post-war notions of policy making, being primarily administrative and organisational in character.

The Education Reform Act was, in contrast, a more fundamental reform, aimed at changing the nature of schooling, through policy intervention in the central area of the curriculum in particular. It brought in a new curricular framework for support and advisory work across the curriculum which was both compulsory and subject-based. In addition the purposes of assessment were extended, with a national system based on norms rather than diagnosis and focused on outputs to evaluate the effectiveness of schools. Although it has been possible to initiate disapplication, generally pupils with special educational needs in mainstream schools have had access to the full National Curriculum and related assessment. This has both changed the nature of curriculum provision for pupils with special needs and widened the role of many SENCOs in schools. There have also been changes in the management framework for SEN. In particular, the delegation of financial management to schools has meant more decision making on SEN at individual school level, with LEA involvement mostly comprising the processes and funding for the small minority of pupils requiring statements. The SENCO has therefore had to learn to work in, manage and balance new national, local and school-based frameworks for policy and provision.

Another particularly significant aspect of this part of policy making over the last 20 years is that although the themes of access and integration have continued, they have often been subsumed within, or been an unintended consequence of, more general reform of education. This is particularly true of the changes which have taken place as a result of the

Education Reform Act. And yet, paradoxically perhaps, the first real basis for future policy making based on an enhanced notion of integration was established through this legislation. The National Curriculum, being in principle designed for all pupils (even though this required a lot of subsequent work for severe learning difficulties and other special needs), can be seen as the first policy realisation of functional (as opposed to just locational or social) integration. It has also ensured that more hidden patterns of segregation, in terms of curricular entitlement in mainstream schools, could not continue, and has legitimated/required the SENCO support role across all subjects. In addition, the reform of educational governance, through local management of schools in particular, has affected not only the general education system but also SEN provision in both mainstream and special schools. As Bowe and Ball (1992) have noted, SEN policy and provision have therefore been brought into both the curriculum and assessment and the market and management frameworks established by the Education Reform Act.

Such integration has of course been problematic as well as beneficial. This is largely because it has been reformulated as standardisation rather than flexibility in terms of the curriculum and related assessment. Notions of 'normal' achievement have been reinforced, leading to more demands for SEN support. At the same time, provision for SEN has been both provided within, and itself subject to, the same themes of competition, diversity, 'consumer' choice and efficiency that the 'market' approach has brought to all education (Bines 1995). There have therefore been considerable pressures on resources, and pressure to market schools as having high achievement, which has made it difficult to put forward SEN as a positive element of schools and realise change. The Code of Practice (DfE 1994) can be seen as an attempt to moderate some of these consequences of marketisation through ensuring more effective and standard implementation of the curricular aspects of reform (Bines and Loxley 1996).

At the same time it is important to consider the extent to which such marketisation has affected fundamentally some important principles and aspects of SEN. Some of the greater excesses of choice and competition have been resisted by schools which, although they might have to compete for pupils and resources, have also wanted to work in clusters and partnerships, particularly in relation to SEN (Lunt et al. 1994). Although the role of the LEA has changed, it has also been preserved, not least through its responsibilities in relation to SEN. Many aspects of school management may have been delegated to schools but some form of holistic education service has remained, which can now be utilised in new ways to establish continuing policy, quality and funding frameworks for the work of the SENCO.

There is still therefore a wider policy context for the SENCO role in particular schools, in the form of the Code of Practice, the re-emerging role of LEAs, and various inter-school partnerships. There are also several policy themes from this period of radical policy making which will continue to inform and shape the future within each school. These include a common compulsory curriculum for all pupils and local management of schools, which will mean both a demanding set of curricular support requirements and a managerial context within which SENCOs will have to continue to argue for SEN provision within the management frameworks of individual schools.

Such an agenda is more than enough to contend with and in itself would be more than sufficient as a basis for the SENCO role of the future. However it would now seem that there are a range of new policy themes emerging which are likely to impact further on the range of the SENCO role. These will now be briefly discussed.

Future policy themes

Inclusion

As evidenced by recent articles in the various SEN journals, new publications in the area of SEN and recent government papers, one of the new policy themes, and possibly the key theme of the future, is inclusion. However, as Clark *et al.* (1997) note, it is not entirely clear what is meant by such a term in either the UK or the international context. Nevertheless, some principles and conceptions are emerging which will be very relevant to SENCO roles in future. The Salamanca statement, for example, which is often quoted as a basis for recent concepts of inclusion, argues that educational systems and programmes should encompass the wide diversity of pupil characteristics and needs and that those pupils with special needs should have access to ordinary schools which must find ways of successfully educating them (Clark *et al.* 1997; Sebba and Ainscow 1996). Such support for inclusion is also found in the recent green paper on SEN (DfEE 1997c), within which inclusion is seen to involve both de-segregation of pupils in special schools and changes in mainstream schools.

This is likely to affect the SENCO role in two ways. Firstly, it is likely that SENCOs will become involved increasingly in a range of inclusion programmes for pupils placed currently in special settings. Secondly, SENCOs will also be expected to reduce the level of statementing and of exclusion of pupils currently in mainstream settings by developing more effective ways of providing for the range of special needs.

Conceptions of inclusion may also influence the SENCO role in other ways. For example, the argument that successful inclusion is dependent on pedagogical and organisational change (Clark *et al*. 1997) may require SENCOs to spend more of their time on such elements of their work. Pedagogical change has of course always been linked closely to making the curriculum more accessible and effective. It may now become even more important, especially given that most of the curriculum is now prescribed through the National Curriculum. Broader engagement with the overall organisation of schools does vary. However, policy and other managerial aspects of the SENCO role, as identified by Dyson (1990, 1991) amongst others, are now becoming far more explicit and are likely to be increasingly important in future.

Equity

The imposition of market principles for education under previous Conservative governments meant that less emphasis was given to equal opportunities and rights. However, inclusion re-asserts the importance of equity as a policy principle for SEN. Nevertheless, establishing what is meant by equity remains problematic. Although principles of equal opportunity remain fundamental to education in the UK, and have underpinned the development of comprehensive primary and secondary schooling, and of initiatives to overcome discrimination in relation to ethnicity and gender, there remains some confusion between liberal (access) and radical (outcomes) elements of the equality debate. This is particularly the case for equal opportunities related to SEN, where it cannot always be assumed that everyone has the same basic capacities and qualities. There is therefore a requirement for a range of positive discrimination measures, such as smaller classes or specialist expertise and resources, if equal access is to result in more equal outcomes from education (Roaf and Bines 1988). Linking equity to certain rights, such as the right to be educated alongside peers, could also strengthen the equity components of SEN policy by linking equity in SEN to wider issues of social justice (ibid.).

However, it is also important to ensure that equal opportunities and rights are not just conceived in general moral terms. Although these may be a key aspect of inclusion, one of the most important reasons for arguing for such an approach is the belief that it will enhance educational potential and outcomes, and thus facilitate more inclusion in adult society. Policy needs to focus on the educational rationales and aspects of equity if it is to be fully meaningful in educational contexts and lead to changes in provision and achievement.

Raising standards

This links clearly to what is likely to be most powerful future policy theme in the next few years, namely raising standards of achievement. This was of course one of the major themes of reform under previous Conservative governments. However, such governments focused on market competition between schools as the main mechanism for improvement, reinforced by the National Curriculum and OFSTED inspection. The Labour government elected in 1997 is tending to focus more on direct educational strategies and on a more collaborative model of change which includes a new role for LEAs in relation to quality assurance and improvement. In addition, whereas policy and provision for SEN was previously marginalised or influenced more by default, it is now being brought explicitly into focus. Above all, it has finally been recognised that pupils who are underachieving or disaffected are often the pupils who are also deemed to have special needs, and that policies to overcome concerns in these areas are often synonymous with, or inextricably linked to, policies for SEN.

This trend is reinforced further through the bringing together of debates and research on SEN and on effective schooling (Ainscow 1991). It is now recognised that each field can benefit from theoretical and practical interaction. Although we are not yet always able to translate the findings of school effectiveness research into school improvement, the tendency of good schools to have a general incorporative approach (Reynolds 1991) would seem to be particularly significant for SEN and for inclusion in particular. Equally, the emphasis in school effectiveness research on the school as an organisation, and on effective staff development and other aspects of management, has particular implications for how the SENCO should work (Ainscow 1991; Clark et al. 1997). The SENCO role is indeed being redefined again, from the original focus on particular pupils and difficulties which then led to wider concerns with curricular and pedagogical change through now to contributing to wider changes in policy, organisation and management in schools. And although SENCOs have always been concerned to raise pupil achievements, they will now be able to focus on such aims within national and local policy contexts that recognise the links between their work and issues of raising achievement in general.

Such developments are illustrated clearly in the green paper on SEN (DfEE 1997c) which indicates how policy and provision for SEN will be brought into wider plans for raising educational achievement in general. There will, for example, be target setting related to SEN, including for pupils in special schools, and it is suggested that the new emphasis on literacy and numeracy will have a direct impact on many of the pupils deemed to have special needs, with the eventual outcome that the number of such pupils may reduce to as low as 10 per cent. It is also hoped that the number of pupils with statements will fall (DfEE 1997c). And although it is recognised that the Code of Practice has generally had a positive effect on policies, planning and provision for SEN (OFSTED 1996, 1997), amendments are likely to be made to reduce paperwork and to focus on the quality of practice in the classroom. The Code of Practice is therefore now also linked explicitly to the agenda of raising standards.

Accountability

Finally, it is important to recognise that SEN policy and provision will continue to be linked to the question of accountability. To date, this has developed in several ways. Firstly there is accountability to parents and pupils as 'consumers' as a result of the market approach to education. Secondly, there will continue to be accountability to both parents and pupils through participation in reviews of, and decisions about, educational provision, notably through the Code of Practice. Thirdly, there is likely to be increasing accountability to both LEAs and government, to ensure that national and local targets and other policy requirements are met, particularly in relation to raising standards. An important document here is the Audit Commission's *Getting the Act Together*, which stresses such accountability and also links it to the requirement for schools to increase their capability to provide for SEN (Audit Commission/HMI 1992). A particular theme in future is likely to be the increased participation of pupils in decisions about their education, to reflect both inclusive principles and the positive impact on educational achievement of such an incorporative approach (Davie 1996). Another is likely to be the growing importance of monitoring and evaluation, not least in relation to the use of funding, which currently is seen as one of the weakest aspects of school policy on SEN and the Code of Practice (OFSTED 1996, 1997). The SENCO, in conjunction with the school as a whole, will have to consider a number of ways of developing such accountability.

Implementing policy

As noted earlier, it is difficult to predict the future. However, we are beginning to see the crystallisation and the convergence of a number of implicit and explicit themes which have dominated SEN and more general education policy since the early 1980s. These can be summarised as centering on quality, capability, equity and accountability (Bines and Thomas 1994) within a national and local policy context that is particularly concerned with raising standards of educational achievement. The task for SENCOs is to identify how they are to be implemented in schools. This will also require some resolution of the contradictory and problematic aspects of such policy themes. Three key questions will need to be asked, namely:

- What should be the fundamental principles of policy?
- How can the school increase its capability for inclusion?
- How can and must the school work with other partners?

Decisions on fundamental principles will involve agreement on whether the school should focus on the moral and ethical aspects of SEN, including equal opportunities and rights, or whether it should gear its policy primarily towards raising educational achievement. Inclusion, of course, involves both, though, as noted earlier, there has been a tendency to emphasise the former. Perhaps this can be resolved by recognising that in addition to rights to be educated alongside peers, pupils with special needs have rights to the highest educational achievements possible. This in turn will only be achieved if the school increases its capability to offer inclusion, through curricular, pedagogical and organisational change, and through an incorporative approach which stresses partnership and participation with pupils, parents and other schools and organisations. Finally, when focusing upon working with others, particular attention will now have to be given to sharing provision, for example with special schools, to sharing policy and practice with other mainstream schools and to sharing planning, particularly with the LEA as it gets more involved again with quality assurance, school development planning and other initiatives such as target setting. More effective working with other professional agencies will also continue to be very important.

For the first time SENCOs are working in a policy climate which has the potential to be really conducive to change. However, the agenda is substantial. It is also contradictory in parts. For example, although inclusion seems to be fundamental to the current government's policies on SEN (DfEE 1997c), it is expected that such inclusion will be implemented within a National Curriculum and associated assessment and achievement targets which are both standardised and inflexible and still do not fully incorporate the needs and progress of some pupils with SEN. In addition, insufficient recognition is being given to other major social factors relevant to underachievement (including SEN), such as poverty and inequality. Further resources are also unlikely.

In addition, as noted elsewhere in this book, despite the impact of the Code of Practice not all schools provide an effective managerial context within which the SENCO can work. For example, time allocated to carry out the role can vary greatly, and in many schools such time may be given primarily to developing Individual Education Plans, rather than working directly with pupils or advising other staff (OFSTED 1996, 1997). Many SENCOs do feel that lack of status, time and resources is impinging on their role and their capacity to implement the Code (Lewis *et al.* 1996). SENCOs are also being increasingly expected to extend their role in relation to behavioural difficulties. The pressures of implementing the SENCO role can therefore be substantial, particularly where the SENCO is responsible for administration and also continues to have a substantial teaching load.

The extent to which SENCOs can actually realise policy intentions is therefore open to question. There will inevitably be policy implementation gaps. There also remains a need for advice and support on implementing SEN policy in general and in the context of individual and particular schools. However, two conclusions can be drawn which may be helpful.

Firstly, it is important to distinguish between what can be termed *strategic* and *operational* policy dimensions and texts. The focus, and the argument, of this chapter is that it is important for SENCOs to appreciate the wider policy trends and contexts within which they work so that they can identify these for their schools. It has been suggested that it will be crucial to review school policy in the light of the growing emphasis on inclusion, standards of pupil achievement, and partnership with, and accountability to, pupils, parents and other bodies such as LEAs. Although the detail of policy is important, operational issues should not dominate thinking. The Code of Practice is but one example of an operational policy text which can take attention away from wider trends and issues through a focus on procedures and paperwork, with problematic consequences. School policies should be concerned with broader issues as well as detail if they are to be effective, and should continue to focus on ethos and principles as well as statutory and other requirements.

Secondly, policy and its implementation should be both open and collaborative, so that issues ranging from funding to curriculum are shared and agreed within the school. Although policy development and advisory and support work with colleagues can be demanding, it does seem that a collective approach is both more effective for the school and less stressful for the SENCO (DfEE 1997b). Above all, such sharing needs to focus on teaching. As Hopkins and Harris have noted (1997), curriculum development has tended to be concerned with content rather than process. A focus on teaching approaches can make schools more successful by both enhancing curricular outcomes and generating a climate of evaluation for improvement. The new commitment to inclusion, with its focus on pedagogical and organisational change, could be a touchstone for such work in school.

Policies for SENCOs

Finally, it is also important to consider policies in relation to the SENCO role itself, and in relation to training and other staff development. An important policy text here is the Teacher Training Agency's draft standards for SENCOs (Teacher Training Agency 1997). Issues of training are discussed elsewhere in this book. However, it should be realised that these standards are in many ways a summary policy text which crystallises many of the issues discussed in terms of detailed expectations of the SENCO. As well as identifying clearly the role of the SENCO in raising educational achievement through improving classroom practice, the standards particularly reinforce and extend the managerial aspects of the SENCO role.

Recognition of the wide range of the role is welcome. However, there remains a narrow focus on basic skills, particularly literacy, which would seem both to define in a very limited way the range of SEN in schools and to run counter to the broader cross-curricular advisory role developed by SENCOs in recent years. There is also an inappropriate level of accountability within which the SENCO is judged by the capabilities of others and the school as a whole. Although the effectiveness of the school is a crucial element of evaluation, the SENCO cannot alone be held responsible for policy and provision for SEN. The collaborative and whole-school aspects of SEN must continue to be emphasised, both to enable improved provision for pupils with SEN and to ensure a realistic evaluation of the SENCO contribution to such work.

It is therefore very important that we continue the debate on the role and the training needs of SENCOs. There should also be national planning to ensure that the required range of training is readily available to both SENCOs and other teachers and professionals concerned with SEN. There is now a requirement that initial training should include various elements on SEN, but this must also be followed through with additional training for class and subject teachers throughout their careers.

The enhancement of opportunity, entitlement and standards of achievement will continue to be key agenda in the development of the SENCO role.

Chapter 3

The problems of interpretation and guidance: the consequences of SENCO action from a legal point of view

William Evans

What is the legal basis for SENCOs' work?

There is no explicit mention of SENCOs in the Education Act. They are not statutory appointments like approved social workers under the Mental Health Acts or monitoring officers under the Local Government and Housing Act 1989. Where, then, in constitutional law terms, do they get their legitimacy from?

The legal trail which leads to the SENCO starts with section 313 of the Education Act 1996. That section says that in discharging their functions under the Act, LEAs, governing bodies and anyone else exercising functions for the purpose of LEAs' or governing bodies' functions, must have regard to the Code of Practice. Paragraphs 2:14 and 2:15 of the Code of Practice recommend the designation in a mainstream school of a teacher (the SEN Coordinator). That coordinator, the SENCO, has the functions listed in paragraph 2:14. As a result, a mainstream school with no SENCO or the equivalent would not be following the Code of Practice. That might be strong evidence that the school had not had regard to the Code of Practice, and was consequently in breach of its duty under section 313 of the 1996 Act.[1]

Under section 313 the SENCO, and others, must 'have regard' to the Code of Practice. What does 'have regard' actually mean? It does not mean 'follow in every detail'. There have been and are similar provisions in other legislation. For example, the Town & Country Planning Acts require a local planning authority, when it considers a planning application, to 'have regard to' certain considerations such as the provisions of the local development plan.[2] What that means has been the subject of court cases.[3] The courts have decided that the authority's obligation is not automatically to follow the provisions of the plan, but to take those provisions into account in coming to a decision. It is almost certain that if a court were faced with a similar dispute about the meaning of section 313 of the Education Act 1996, it would interpret it similarly.

What is the legal context in which SENCOs work?

Like most professionals, whatever their discipline, SENCOs work simultaneously within several legal frameworks:

- they are employees, so they have rights and obligations under the terms of their contracts of employment;
- they are subject to the requirements of the articles of government of the school in which they work;
- they are required by section 313 of the Education Act 1996 to have regard to the provisions of the Code of Practice;
- they are subject to, and have the benefit of, the various provisions relating to their work in the Education Act and in the regulations and other subordinate legislation made under the Act;
- they, and their employers, are subject to the general law of the land, but particularly as regards negligence and breach of statutory duty.

Consequently, as with most professional disciplines, the scope for ambiguity, inconsistency and conflict is generous.

The SENCO's contract of employment

In a maintained school, the SENCO will be subject to the standard general obligations listed in the Teachers' Pay and Conditions Orders, which apply to all teachers in maintained schools. Subject to that, the SENCO will be bound by the terms of his or her own contract of employment with the SENCO's employer. The employer may be the LEA or the governing body of the school, depending on what sort of school it is. The contract of employment will usually be in local standard form. It may incorporate terms and conditions from other documents, in particular from collective agreements negotiated, nationally or locally, between the employer or an employers' organisation and recognised trade unions or professional associations, and adopted by the employer. It may include a job description, which may spell out in more or less detail some of the SENCO's obligations, or at least indicate the employer's expectations of what the SENCO is to do; it may also define some of the SENCO's powers: it might mention, for example, reporting relationships, management responsibilities, or delegated power to commit resources.

In common law an employee is obliged to comply with any lawful requirements the employer makes within the terms of the contract of employment. Apart from instructions on particular occasions, that imports into the contract (a) the employer's standard requirements about things like management structure, resource allocation, and administrative procedures (including in particular the way the teacher gets authority to commit the school to spending money); and (b) the internal management arrangements for the school, which the head teacher has the right to determine under the articles of government of the school. The SENCO is contractually obliged to work within the operational procedures lawfully thus set by the LEA, the governing body and the head teacher.

Apart from any practical effects such as chaos, non-compliance with the terms of the SENCO's contract of employment can have two legal effects. First, as between the SENCO and the employer, the breach could lead to action under the school's grievance or disciplinary procedures, and in an extreme case to dismissal. Secondly, as regards third parties such as parents, the fact that something has been done outside the terms of the SENCO's contract of employment may raise the question of whether the SENCO had legal power to do the act in question, and thus may provide grounds for legal proceedings to challenge or quash what has been decided or done.

The articles of government of the school

One of the legal functions of the articles of government of a school is to demarcate, in broad terms, who can decide what. Some decisions are allocated to the LEA, some to the governing body, and some to the head teacher. Articles of government are made under one section or other of the Education Act, and are therefore a form of delegated legislation, so in constitutional law terms they have, broadly speaking, the same effect as an Act of Parliament. Given that a SENCO's contract of employment is of little practical meaning except in the context of the statutory education system, the provisions of the articles of government of a school, and what they imply, would probably also be treated by a court as deemed to be incorporated into a teacher's contract of employment.

The constitutional significance of the articles of government is that where they allocate power to make a particular type of decision to one person or body, then (a) that function cannot be usurped by anyone else; (b) any decision taken by someone who has not been allocated the power to do it is legally void and of no legal effect; and (c) it is not lawful for the person or body charged with a particular responsibility to duck that responsibility by allowing or arranging for someone else to make that decision, unless the articles or the Act give explicit power to do so. Any decision that does not observe those rules is open to legal challenge.

The Code of Practice

The legal status of the Code of Practice is like other codes of practice, such as the Highway Code, the approved codes of practice for health and safety at work, the codes of practice issued by the Advisory, Conciliation and Arbitration Service on employment practices, and those published by the relevant Commissions on sex, race and disability discrimination. You do not commit a criminal offence or a breach of the civil law simply by infringing or ignoring a recommendation in the Code of Practice. But (a) if a decision is made in complete disregard of what the Code of Practice says on the subject, then the decision is open to legal challenge because section 313 of the Education Act 1996 says that anyone exercising functions for the purposes of LEAs' or governing bodies' functions (which is what SENCOs do) must have regard to the Code of Practice; and (b) any departure from the Code of Practice can be taken into account by a court or tribunal in deciding any relevant issue. So a departure from the Code of Practice can be evidence towards proving, for example, that an assessment was inadequate, or that provision is not appropriate.

Negligence and breach of statutory duty

Put over-simply, the law of negligence imposes a duty of care on organisations and individuals towards those with whom they have certain relationships and who can reasonably be foreseen to be likely to suffer injury or damage which is reasonably foreseeable as the likely consequence of an act or omission by the organisation or individual. Break that duty of care, and you can be sued for damages to compensate.

A competent teacher acting with common sense and in accordance with recognised and accepted good professional practice is unlikely to have much cause to be worried about being sued for negligence. If a teacher is sued for negligence, the bill is almost certain to be picked up by the teacher's employer, because the employer is vicariously liable for what the teacher does in the course of the teacher's employment. Most employers insure against liability both for themselves and their employees as individuals. Irrespective of legal considerations, however, most teachers will wish to avoid putting themselves into a position of being sued in the first place.

It has long been settled law that a teacher owes certain duties of care to pupils and students. Most of the reported cases spring from allegations of lack of physical care resulting in physical injury or death, but it is also now well established that damage to mental health can be sued for, so long as it amounts to a recognised psychiatric illness.[4] Outside the context of a school, it is possible in certain circumstances to sue for economic loss, particularly where that has been caused by negligent advice or negligent mis-statement of facts which the victim has reasonably relied on.[5] The courts have not yet decided whether that principle would allow a child in an appropriate case to win damages for loss of career prospects, but by analogy with decided cases against doctors for medical professional negligence, there seems no reason in principle why, in an appropriate case, a parent should not be able to recover damages for things like the cost of remedial provision, medical treatment, and other expenses which the parent or child would not have had to pay for had the defendant not been negligent. A number of solicitors' firms, some using legally-aided children and parents as plaintiffs, are seeking to bring test cases so as to get the courts to clarify not only the categories of expenditure for which damages can be claimed, but also the extent to which local education authorities can be held liable for negligence or other default in the way they meet pupils' and students' special educational needs. In one case the High Court has awarded damages of £37,000 against a local education authority for what the court held to be negligent failure by an educational psychologist to diagnose specific learning difficulties.[6]

The circumstances in which an action can be brought for shortcomings in the detection, assessment and remediation of special educational needs is still being argued in the courts, but a number of principles, some of them still emerging, can be indicated. First, the courts are treating differently cases where the claim alleges that the local authority is in breach of its statutory duty, and cases where the allegation is that an employee of the authority has been negligent in delivering, or failing to deliver, a service to the child.[7]

Secondly, a school or an individual teacher is likely to be adjudged to owe a more stringent duty of care towards pupils with particular types of learning difficulty than towards the average pupil. SENCOs will be familiar with this principle from their health and safety responsibilities, and the general principle that in schools, like any other premises, one must expect children to be less careful than adults: all the more so where a child is known to be exceptionally vulnerable.[8] Thirdly, the courts are likely to regard a SENCO as having a higher duty than the average teacher towards such pupils, because the SENCO is more likely, by reason of role, specialisation and experience, to be more aware of such pupils' vulnerabilities.[9]

Fourthly, the courts are beginning to treat codes of practice published by professional bodies as setting the standard below which an act may be considered negligent: one such case was about accountancy standards,[10] but there seems no reason in principle why the same should not apply to other professions: all the more so where the code of practice is drawn up and published, not by the ruling professional body (there is none at the moment for teachers), but by the government department responsible for the service overall. Lastly, the courts will take into account evidence of good practice, where it is published, widespread and accepted, as benchmarks for deciding whether a particular action or lack of it is negligent: so the court is likely to be influenced by publications such as the Department for Education and Employment's *The SENCO Guide*, published in September 1997, including the warning in the Introduction that not all the ideas mentioned are necessarily appropriate for every school.

On the other hand, the courts seem more ready to recognise that public authorities need to have freedom in exercising discretionary powers, especially where professional judgement is involved: the courts have long recognised the need to respect doctors' clinical judgment,[11] and there are signs that this respect is being extended to decisions by members of other professions.

At the same time the courts are more ready to recognise that public authorities' resources are limited, so that large awards of damages, and the consequential higher premiums, restrict public authorities' ability to deliver the services parliament has required them to provide. Observing perhaps the growth of defensive medicine in the United States, the courts have acknowledged in several cases involving a range of public services that it is not in the public interest for authorities providing large-scale public services to be driven by negligence awards into 'defensive' practices.[12] And in the context of the law of local authority social services, the courts have held that whilst there may be cases where the carelessness of a social worker could give rise to liability, it would generally be contrary to public policy for a social worker exercising parental responsibilities with regard to a child being looked after by a local authority to be made subject to a common law duty of care and thus exposed to the risk of claims for professional negligence.[13]

The Bedfordshire appeals

Several of these issues were considered by the House of Lords in a batch of cases reported under *X* v. *Bedfordshire County Council* and other appeals.[14] The Bedfordshire case itself was about how the council as local social services authority and its social services department staff had responded to allegations of child abuse, but three of the other appeals involved claims for damages alleging breach of statutory duty and common law negligence in various aspects of the detection and assessment of learning difficulties and the making of provision to meet special educational needs. Whilst it was SEN managers, educational psychologists and related staff whose conduct was being attacked, the principles laid down by the court will apply equally to SENCOs.

In *E* v. *Dorset County Council* the plaintiff was a primary school pupil with specific learning difficulties. Dissatisfied with the provision made by the LEA, his parents moved him to a private school, and sought to recover, among other things, the cost. A specific allegation was that the LEA's educational psychologist had negligently advised the parents.

In *Christmas* v. *Hampshire County Council* the plaintiff was a primary school pupil with behavioural and specific learning difficulties. The head teacher had denied that the child had any specific learning difficulties, and that view was supported by the LEA's internal specialist advisory service. The claim was that the head teacher was negligent in failing to refer the child for assessment, and that the advisory service staff had been negligent in carrying out their assessment, in failing to diagnose, and in failing to refer to an educational psychologist. 'As a result the plaintiff had been disadvantaged in reaching his potential and his vocational opportunities and prospects significantly restricted.'

The issue before the House of Lords in all these appeals was not whether the LEA staff had been negligent, but whether the claim should be struck out at the outset as showing no cause of action at all.

The House of Lords decided that a local authority is not liable in negligence simply because it has carelessly exercised or failed to exercise a statutory power: the plaintiff has to show that the LEA owed the plaintiff a duty of care at common law. In particular, the House of Lords decided that the LEA will not be held liable for the negligent exercise of a statutory discretion involving policy considerations. That judgement is consistent with the constitutional principle that the courts will not interfere with or hold unlawful the exercise of a statutory discretion where to do so would amount to the court substituting its own decision for that of the body to which parliament has given the power to make the decision, especially where the body concerned is democratically elected.

The House of Lords decided however that where there is a proximate relationship between a LEA employee and the plaintiff, such as that between educational psychologist and pupil (all the more so, one would expect, between teacher and pupil having personal contact several hours a day most days of the working week), then a duty of care is owed to the pupil. The House of Lords held in both the Dorset and the Hampshire cases that the claims should not be struck out in so far as they alleged negligence by individual employees delivering the service direct to the pupil.

How far the courts will develop that line in cases involving special educational needs is not yet clear, but the case of *Phelps* v. *Hillingdon LBC* in September 1997 shows that the High Court is prepared to hold individual educational psychologists liable for negligence in not detecting learning difficulties.

The result of the case-law at present appears to be that

- a parent or child cannot sue an LEA for damages simply for negligent exercise of discretion, especially where the decision is taken in a policy context, and that may include decisions for budgetary or operational reasons to ration a particular service, to rank pupils according to priority of need, or to establish a waiting list;
- a child, and possibly a parent, may be able to sue an individual employee of a local authority, such as a SENCO, for negligence in discharge of the employer's day-to-day functions provided directly to the individual child, where the LEA, the governing body or the SENCO owes a duty of care to that particular child because of the proximate relationship between the school and the child the school has enrolled, or between the professional and the child receiving the service the professional is employed to deliver to or with respect to the child;
- a SENCO may be legally liable to a child, and possibly to a parent as well, for negligently giving incorrect advice to the parent in circumstances where the SENCO must have known that the parent was going to rely on that advice, and did so to the child's, and possibly their own, detriment or loss;

- an LEA may be liable where it has statutory powers in the background which allow it to apply a sanction to the parents, such as a school attendance order or prosecution, and threatens to use them if the parent does not adopt a course of action which the LEA or its employee, such as a SENCO, negligently prescribes.

What guidance in the Code of Practice refers to the SENCO?

The Code of Practice needs to be looked at as a whole, for several reasons. First, the Code is as much about attitudes, purposes and approaches as about rules, and that can be missed if the Code is read line by line. Secondly, it may be misleading to refer to paragraphs in isolation, because what the SENCO does is done in a context to which other professionals, acting with other paragraphs of the Code in mind, contribute. A SENCO can hardly perform properly if ignorant of what the Code calls for from, for example, the LEA's central support services. Other professionals similarly will act in the expectation that SENCOs themselves will act in accordance with those provisions of the Code that relate to them. Thirdly, the Code seeks to offer guidance to all types and sizes of mainstream school, and it does not always differentiate for schools which may have particular circumstances or needs. The SENCO for a small rural aided primary school and the SENCO in a large inner-city comprehensive face different problems, not just in terms of numbers and scale.

Even so, it may be helpful to go through the Code and pick out the paragraphs that refer to the SENCO. They are as follows.

2:14 lists key functions of the SENCO. A useful exercise might be to compare this list (which is summarised on page 4 of *The SENCO Guide*) with the SENCO's job description, if any. There needs to be a good reason if any of the functions in 2:14 are not mentioned in the job description. That someone else has responsibility for a particular task might be a good reason.

2:15 makes the point that in a large school SENCO responsibilities may require a team, not just one designated individual. Where responsibilities are split, there needs to be communication and coordination, perhaps management. Do the management arrangements for the school require, allow and facilitate that?

2:59 says that SENCOs should be aware of the LEA's policy on support services, and how to tap them. Does the SENCO have that information?

Have training or information needs been surveyed? Is there administrative machinery for the dissemination of information from the LEA centre and feedback from the school? Is the SENCO free to approach the NHS direct, or is there a particular route or procedure for communication?

2:61–120 describe the school-based stages for identification, assessment, monitoring and review of pupils with special educational needs but no statement. Roles are ascribed to the SENCO, e.g. receiving information from the class teacher under Stage 1 and registering it (2:65, 74 and 75); coordinating Stage 2 provision (2:66, with a list of activities); leading (2:85) and coordinating under Stage 2 (2:67, with an action list at 2:86 to 93); drawing up the child's individual education programme (2:93 with checklist); fixing the review (2:95) and conducting it (2:96, with checklist); choosing review outcomes (2:97); triggering Stage 3 (2:100); continuing to lead under Stage 3 (2:101) and informing the LEA (2:102); getting the information (2:103); calling in the specialist support (2:104–105 and 107); writing the Stage 3 IEP (2:108, 112 with checklist); arranging reviews (2:113); recording outcomes (2:115); and advising on the procedures for statutory assessment; being consulted by other people, e.g. the class teacher under 2:77 and 80; consulting others, e.g. under 2:78 as to whether a child should remain on the register. In these functions, the legal questions are whether the school's and the LEA's management arrangements, and in particular the arrangements for communication and dissemination of information, are such as to allow the SENCO to do all this. Within a school, resource allocation and timetabling may be an issue.

3:53 describes the SENCO's role in the formal assessment process. Similar considerations apply.

4:54 mentions the SENCO's role when the LEA decides not to name the parent's choice of school in Part 4 of the statement.

5:29 ascribes a role to the SENCO when a child enters primary school, with checklist.

6:10 thoughtfully mentions the SENCO as one of the people to be considered for invitation to attend the child's annual review.

What does this guidance imply? The Code of Practice addresses a large tract of the special educational needs function, and it takes context for granted, so understandably it sometimes reads as if the SENCO is autonomous. A SENCO operates in a school, and is subject to all the constraints that entails, not just the legal constraints mentioned above. At least the Code of Practice acknowledges (2:15) that a SENCO's timetable needs to have regard to the school's resources and the guidance in the Code; it might rather have said that when setting the SENCO's timetable the school needs to have regard to the resource implications of the Code of Practice.

In particular, the risk of legal problems can be reduced if the following points are addressed:

- The SENCO needs to be identified and the SENCO's role needs to be explained to other staff.
- Class teachers need to be told of their responsibility to consult, and to pass information to, the SENCO. This responsibility must include updating.
- There needs to be a system whereby the SENCO can disseminate information among, or direct it to, other staff.
- The SENCO needs a system for recording information about children.
- SENCOs' training needs need to be identified and met.
- SENCOs may need to train, or to participate in the training of, other staff.
- If not a member of the school's management team, the SENCO needs access to it.
- The SENCO needs information about the LEA's support services and systems, and their contact and access points. This information needs constant updating.
- The SENCO needs similar information about support services external to the LEA, e.g. social services, the NHS and voluntary agencies.
- The SENCO needs a system for diarying review dates, deadlines and such like.

If the above, as a minimum, is not in place, then there is a risk that the SENCO role will not be discharged properly. That may lead to the child not receiving the attention, the assessment and the provision that is the child's legal and moral entitlement. That may lead to complaints, perhaps formal complaints to the local government ombudsman, or even claims for breach of statutory duty or for negligence. This is particularly important when the child is within Stage 2 or Stage 3 of the Code of Practice, because it is at those stages that the Code of Practice says that it is the SENCO who should be leading the various activities.

Another approach might be to review practice in the light of the more generalised key questions posed in paragraph 1:22 of *The SENCO Guide*.

A SENCO who can give affirmative answers to all those questions need have no fear of legal action being successful.

Notes

1. For academic critiques of the use of codes of practice as instruments of government, see for example Ganz 1987, Galligan 1986.
2. Town & Country Planning Act 1990 s.70(2).
3. *Simpson* v. *Edinburgh Corporation* 1960 SC 313, HL; *Enfield LBC* v. *Secretary of State for the Environment* [1975] JPL 155; *Co-op Retail Services* v. *Taff-Ely BC* (1979) 39 P&CR 1, CA; affirmed (1981) 42 P&CR 1, HL.
4. *Hinz* v. *Berry* [1970] 2 QB 40, [1970] 1 All ER 1074, CA.
5. *Hedley Byrne* v. *Heller* [1964] AC 465, [1963] 2 All ER 575, HL.
6. *Phelps* v. *Hillingdon LBC*, *Guardian* 24 September 1997, QBD.
7. *X* v. *Bedfordshire County Council* [1995] 2 AC 633, [1995] 3 All ER 353, HL.
8. *Glasgow Corporation* v. *Taylor* [1922] 1 AC 44, HL.
9. *Knight* v. *Home Office* [1990] 3 All ER 237.
10. *Lloyd Cheyham* v. *Littlejohn* [1987] BCLC 303, [1986] PCC 389.
11. *Maynard* v. *West Midlands* RHA [1985] 1 All ER 635.
12. For example, *Hill* v. *Chief Constable of W. Yorkshire* [1989] AC 53, [1988] 2 All ER 238, HL.
13. *Barrett* v. *Enfield LBC*, *The Times* 22 April 1997; *Law Society's Gazette* 94/17 30 April 1997, CA.
14. [1995] 2 AC 633; [1995] 3 All ER 353.

Chapter 4

SENCOs and the Code: no longer practising

John Dwyfor Davies, Philip Garner and John Lee

Since the Education Reform Act of 1988, teachers have often felt that they have had to carry out their work in a climate characterised by criticism from both government and society in general. Compulsory education, including that of children who have special educational needs in England and Wales remains under close scrutiny. Official inspection and its results are widely publicised, particularly when a school is identified as 'failing'. There is also a perception that many of the decisions made in respect of practice seldom incorporate contributions from classroom teachers or middle managers (i.e. those who interact most frequently with children). Negative comments from the Chief Inspector have also made a significant contribution to the decline in morale, and serve to amplify a widespread feeling amongst teachers that their work is often misunderstood or undervalued. What is almost paradoxical is that the government has, in mid-1998, set out on a policy pathway aimed at raising the status of teachers – which is rather like Genghis Khan having a sympathetic cup of tea with one of his victims.

The impact of the Code of Practice has meant a significant increase in workload and a reorientation in working practices, a situation which has been well documented in recent and emergent literature (Dyson and Gains 1995; Stakes and Hornby 1997). Elsewhere there have been a number of studies which have provided substantial data, both quantitative and qualitative, concerning the ways in which SENCOs have adjusted to this new situation (Lewis 1995, Garner 1996). For the purposes of this chapter however, we intend to use a number of ways of exploring the views of SENCOs in respect of their recall of the work that they have been doing over the last year or so. In a sense, therefore, the insights provided are one indication of the maturing role of the SENCO and the gradual sophistication in the ways in which they have adapted their management function as a result of experience.

How was it for you?

Many of the ongoing concerns felt by SENCOs can be investigated when such teachers first embark on award-bearing professional development courses in special educational needs. Acknowledging both passionate commitment and a perceived feeling of isolation and professional uncertainty requires great personal courage and risk-taking. One way in which this has been tackled is by the use of graphical representation (Garner, Hinchcliffe and Sandow, 1995), which offers a non-threatening way of uncovering such feelings.

To provide an example of this approach we will draw upon the work of one SENCO, who was asked to represent her thoughts about her job in the form of a drawing or diagram. The teacher had just begun a 15-week professional development module entitled 'Management and Special Needs'. She was asked to provide this graphical information in such a way as to give an unfamiliar observer some insight about her position as SENCO in her school, the way in which SEN was managed and the relationship between herself and her colleagues. The teacher was also asked to provide a brief written explanation of her drawing. In the case described, confidentiality has been maintained by providing the contributing SENCO with a fictitious name.

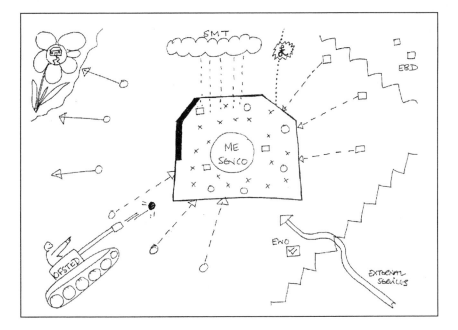

Figure 4.1 Concept map

Sally Mowbray's 'concept map' reveals substantial information concerning the way in which she sees her role as SENCO in a medium-sized primary school. Sally is in her eighth year as a teacher, and Bond Park Primary School is her second teaching post. Even without her commentary it is possible to deduce some of the tensions which are apparent in managing SEN provision in the late-1990s. As an experiment, and with Sally's permission, a colleague who has worked in art therapy was asked to give some impressions as to what it meant. Lynda, the therapist, responded by saying:

> This person is clearly displaying quite a bit of controlled anger and aggression. The arrows, military images and jagged lines suggest this. But the drawing is robust and clear, indicating to me that this person is very determined and single-minded in what she does. I'm not sure what the crosses mean. As I have a contact who works in special education I can say that 'me = SENCO' within a circle is very indicative. It suggests to me that she is highly involved with her work, almost dangerously so.

Sally Mowbray agreed wholeheartedly with some of these observations. She said that it was '...true that I am a hundred per cent committed to the job, and equally that I'm very angry – I wouldn't say especially controlled – about what has happened to SEN, especially about the funding of it'. She also indicated some annoyance at the therapist's inference that she was her job, Sally defiantly stating that she was '...definitely not a sad person'!

She begins her written commentary on her drawing by stating that she saw her role as complex in terms of the number and range of individuals she had to interact with. She felt some frustration that she could only partly control the quality of this interaction – especially in the case of some of her teaching colleagues and the external support services. She commented that:

> There are so many people to see, often in the space of just a few moments at the start of the day. I can't keep notes, because these aren't timetabled meetings. So it's like a juggling exercise and I like to think I can keep things in my head alright. The worst thing is you are so often reliant on how other people receive what you are telling them (or discussing with them), and we've got at least two people at Bond Park who simply don't want to know. Your therapist is right in one way about my anger – I'm angry at them, because they make everybody else's job that more difficult, but especially mine.

In describing the content of her drawing Sally gave the following explanation:

> I am in the middle – that's how I see it – surrounded by my children (these are the crosses), the teachers who really support me (they're the circles), the cooperative parents (the squares). I see this definitely as a little empire. It's not something I have set out to do, but I've had to do it to survive.

Sally then went on to explain in some detail a range of difficulties she encountered in her role as SENCO at the school. She said that the thick black line in the drawing represented the barrier '…between me and some other teachers…who seem out of date and at least one of them can't wait to leave'. The circles and squares joined by dotted lines to 'the empire' represent, according to Sally, those teachers and parents who are usually cooperative, but who need '…quite a bit of pushing to do things'. The parents of several children who had behaviour problems were very hard to reach, and therefore Sally portrayed them in her drawing as being separated by a barrier.

The senior management team, Sally maintained, were often '…in a cloud, because of lots of external pressures, like league tables and things not connected with the internal working of the school. Sometimes they are unable to stop the pressures getting through to me, so that's where the rain seeps in!' The only support agency with which Sally felt there was an effective relationship was the educational welfare officer (EWO), with other services being too 'distant' to be of much use. Thus Sally observed that:

> I find the most frustrating thing about being SENCO is that people think you've got lots of time to go to meetings. This isn't so, and I get very annoyed when I see how little contact I have with our educational psychologist – mainly because it is so worthwhile when I get to meet with her.

Sally reserves the most symbolic image in her drawing for OFSTED – which she portrays as a tank firing a cannonball.

> This really sums up what I think and what other SENCOs in the area believe'. There seems to be so little support, so little feedback, and in return about two months of our routines are completely wrecked. It doesn't make sense. Soon they'll be frightening the children.

As a contrast, there is a hint of pastoral peace and quiet in the top left-hand corner of the drawing. Sally says that this is '…my home, where I can retire to lick my wounds, begin to feel optimistic again, stroke the cat and get ready to begin another day'.

It has been noted, even prior to the implementation of the Code, that many teachers of children with learning difficulties feel a sense of discomfort at becoming managers of people rather than teachers of children *per se* (Dyson 1991). Sally's concept map provides some evidence of her struggle in this respect, a role-reorientation which is being undertaken in a context of structural change to the education service as a whole, a phenomenon also supported by the findings of quantitative work relating to the function of SENCOs (Lewis 1995).

There is, of course, a danger in using a graphical device such as this. Often SENCOs can become preoccupied with a negative interpretation of their role, as a result of the acknowledged pressure they are under. Drawings such as Sally's, however, can be used in a very constructive manner. They can help provide an institutional overview (albeit a highly personalised one) of possible strengths and weaknesses in provision. Thus, several SENCOs have used this method in school-based professional development sessions, with some highly positive results. Participants in these exercises indicated that they had a wide range of interpretations of the function of the SENCO in their school and of the overall way in which SEN was managed. This then allowed staff to locate areas where further professional development could be targeted.

SENCO: the hub – even if the wheel's falling off

St Michael's Primary School is a large, successful primary school in an outer London borough. The number of pupils on roll is 280. The school provides education across the ability range as prescribed by the National Curriculum. Within its neighbourhood the school has a good reputation, and has secured high ratings from OFSTED. It has always secured a position within the top half of the 'league tables' [sic] which are viewed by some as representing the true educational performance of schools.

St Michael's is staffed by 11 teachers, including the head teacher. Provision for SEN, from September 1997, comprised a SENCO and 0.5 classroom assistants designated to support nine children with statements. In addition, a teacher was made available from the LEA's Speech and Language Service on a half-day per week basis. The school had recently (August 1997) designated a governor to oversee SEN matters. A yearly sum of £350.00 was allocated for SEN resources.

Mary Bradley, the school's SENCO, had indicated a wish to focus on an audit of SEN provision as a topic for her Masters degree, which she was currently undertaking at a local university's school of education. Following the agreement of the school's governing body she decided to examine the progress made by the school since its last (successful) OFSTED inspection in 1994, at a time just after the publication of the draft Code of Practice. This inspection noted a number of positive aspects of provision, notably that several classroom teachers were already proactive in the production of differentiated resources. It was also noted that this same group of teachers had for SEN developed effective working relationships with the SENCO, and that plans were already in place to implement IEPs.

It was Mary Bradley's belief that a lot had been done by the staff to implement the Code of Practice, and that things were '…generally running quite smoothly with the occasional hiccups along the way'. Nevertheless, she had some concerns. She was uneasy that no-one had really conducted an institutional appraisal of the way in which SEN was being managed, resulting in her feeling that '…some of my colleagues think that they can sit back on the basis of an inspection over two years ago. A lot of water has gone under the bridge since then, and we need to re-evaluate the situation quite urgently.'

Mary's audit incorporated a number of data-gathering devices, including:

- Discussion with all SEN-related staff (including classroom assistants and external professionals).
- Analysis of school documents relating to SEN.
- Interviews with classroom teachers.
- Interview with members of the senior management team.
- Interview with school governor responsible for SEN.

The results of the audit, as well as providing the basis for Mary's successful completion of her MA, had significant institutional benefits. It identified the nature of continuing good practice on the part of some classroom teachers, the refinements made to the school's SEN policy documents since their implementation in 1995, and the positive leadership provided by the SMT on SEN matters. On the other hand, the audit uncovered a set of concerns which Mary was subsequently to address during a series of INSET sessions.

SEN was perceived as a 'subject' by several classroom teachers and by many of the classroom assistants

The school's staff handbook itself identified special needs as a separate entity, thus failing to convey the role of SEN colleagues as advisors/facilitators and support workers across all disciplines. Mary noted that there was an inherent weakness in the current written special needs policy of the school, in that it failed to identify clearly the responsibilities of individual classroom teachers in respect of Stage 1 of the Code of Practice. She also noted that, in a diagrammatic representation of line management for the school as a whole, SEN was identified as a separate component. This, Mary thought, simply serves to maintain a perception that SEN is a self-contained 'department'.

Consequently, whilst some classroom teachers were aware of the advisory role of the SENCO, and of their own individual responsibilities in meeting Level 1 learning difficulties, this perception was variable. Some colleagues were inclined to see the pupil with learning difficulties as the sole responsibility of the SENCO herself, resulting in Mary's work '…assuming the proportions of a mountain in certain classes in the school' and leaving her with a feeling that '…those teachers who do least for SEN pupils get most of my time. It is hardly fair.'

SEN pupils were frequently identified as a threat rather than as a resource

Several teachers interviewed suggested that, contrary to the NCC's *A Curriculum for All* (NCC 1989), which maintains that the starting point for intervention with SEN pupils is a recognition of the strengths that they bring to the learning situation, they were frequently seen in problematic terms. One classroom teacher commented that '…if I didn't have to spend such a lot of time on my SENs [sic] I am sure that all of the other children would achieve higher scores.' The same teacher expressed almost relief at the prospect of certain children with learning difficulties being withdrawn from her class so that '…she could get on with her job'. Mary's audit found a similar view being presented by two other teachers.

Some classroom teachers were unaware of their responsibilities under Stage 1 of the Code of Practice; others were unfamiliar with the Code's wider implications

Three of the teachers Mary interviewed did not appear to be fully conversant with Stage 1 of the Code of Practice or their role in the staged assessment/intervention process. This made for complications for example when considering transfer from Stage 1 to Stage 2. Whilst all of the teachers in the school were familiar with the Code of Practice as a physical document, less than half expressed familiarity with its basic contents as they related to their own role in assessment and intervention. Few of the classroom assistants were familiar with the Code.

IEPs were seen as the responsibility of the SEN Coordinator: little input from classroom teachers appeared to be forthcoming

The audit revealed evidence of occupational overload on the SENCO in St Michael's Primary School, notably in managing IEPs. The absence of a clearly articulated policy statement regarding the statutory responsibilities of all classroom teachers in respect of SEN tended to make this situation inevitable. Mary believed that the role of SENCO should be more about management and, as the title implies, coordination. Yet there was evidence in the audit that this function was being marginalised because the SENCO was required to intervene directly in SEN matters at Stages 1 and 2 as a result of the failure of some classroom teachers to fulfil their responsibilities. This situation did not seem to allow for an effective utilisation of the skills and experience of the SENCO, nor for cost-effectiveness, given the level of Mary's seniority and experience.

The audit's findings were particularly revealing in respect of IEP construction and maintenance. Two classroom teachers' comments were indicative of a highly negative view: 'I think that IEPs are a waste of my time and I think they are also unfair. Why should a child who continually misbehaves have all of that time spent on him? I haven't got the time, and isn't that what a SENCO is paid for anyway?'; 'There are loads of other things that get in the way of me doing the IEPs, and I think in any case that Mary's in a better position to write them herself...she knows the kids she's dealing with.'

There appeared to be no explicit rationale for the choice of withdrawal or in-class support

Mary's audit showed that the school as a whole held mixed views about the value of in-class support compared to withdrawal. Some of the class teachers she spoke to said that in-class support could only work provided that the quality of the support worker could be assured. A more militant approach was adopted by one teacher who stated that 'It is better if they [sic] are taken out of class; they will get specialised 1:1 attention and I can get on with my job. Everybody benefits.' The choice of withdrawal or in-class support also appeared to be made on an *ad hoc* basis, rather than upon an explicit and rational analysis of individual learning needs.

Mary Bradley's SEN audit was not simply a paper exercise. It resulted in a set of recommendations for future action to the SMT of St Michael's: at the time of writing each of these is being addressed. Looking back on the exercise, Mary felt that she had also uncovered a number of hitherto unacknowledged features in the way she had been working with her colleagues in the school. Examining SEN provision in the school as a whole had thus allowed her to define key aspects of her own operational style – in some senses she had undertaken a form of self-appraisal. Her overriding feeling was that she was still being required to do too much of what she referred to as 'fetching and carrying', and she believed that, '...whilst I'm the hub of the SEN action in the school I feel as though pressure of work is causing me to lose contact with the rest of the wheel.'

Although it would be wrong to say that progress has not been made since the advent of the Code of Practice, it is also the case that each of the themes identified in Mary's audit tells us something about the fragile nature of a SENCO's work. The concerns expressed in 1998 are an accurate approximation of those voiced in the first year of the Code's implementation. Thus, SENCOs still express grave reservations about IEPs, about the logistics of internal collaboration, about the process of inclusion and about the degree to which the failure of many schools to operationalise the good intentions of whole-school SEN policies results in immense, and frequently avoidable, pressure. Each of these issues is now further examined utilising some data drawn from a small-scale survey of primary SENCOs.

The views of SENCOs

Ten SENCOs in three outer London primary schools were invited to participate, with the agreement of their head teachers, in a semi-structured conversation concerning the way in which, after three years experience of working to the Code, they exercised their management duties. The data-gathering procedure adopted was similar to that used elsewhere (see Garner 1995). The SENCOs were identified opportunistically, with eight out of the ten having each recently completed an in-service SEN module provided by a local university. Each of the SENCOs had between five and twelve years of teaching experience, apart from one who was in only the second year of her teaching career. The gender imbalance, arguably one of the most notable personnel characteristics in primary schools, was significant: just one of the SENCOs was male. Indicative of pressures referred to by Lewis (1995), all of the SENCOs in this study were also class teachers.

A semi-structured conversation schedule was adapted from some of the findings of the second report on the implementation of the Code of Practice (OFSTED 1997) and from collaborative work with a local SENCO (Mary Bradley – see above). It asked for the SENCOs' views on four issues which both the official report and the local audit had identified as central to the effective management of SEN: the use of IEPs, logistics of internal collaboration, attitudes to inclusion and whole-school SEN policies. The schedule contained 12 main questions, supported by a series of subsidiary questions. Each conversation lasted about 60 minutes, and involved three SENCOs discussing the themes highlighted in the conversation schedule. The SENCOs were subsequently able to examine the transcript of their conversation, and given the opportunity to erase, amend or substantiate any of their comments. In order to preserve the anonymity of contributors each was given an alias and all other real names were changed.

Each of the following four sections is not intended to provide an exhaustive coverage of what the SENCOs had to say about particular topics. Rather, the verbatim comments and the accompanying summaries provide a further indication of the complexity of a SENCO's work.

SEN Coordinators' views on the use of IEPs

The SENCOs in this study were concerned about two aspects of IEPs: the involvement of colleagues and of the pupils themselves in their construction and maintenance and the increased workload that IEPs brought with them. Both of these concerns were highlighted in OFSTED's second report on the Code. The report noted that 'The preparation and maintenance of IEPs is the area of greatest concern for the majority of schools' (OFSTED 1997), although it did infer that IEPs were somewhat easier to implement in primary schools: 'These tasks are more manageable in primary schools; there is greater agreement amongst staff about the IEP format and the arrangements for reviewing an IEP' (ibid.). Nine of the ten SENCOs interviewed for this chapter supported the first observation, but all disagreed with the second. Mary, for example, said that 'In our school there are at least two teachers who always fail to provide information, always find some way of avoiding attending meetings; all this means is that I have to scream around to get the information in time I could spend doing other things.' Nathalie, in supporting this viewpoint, felt that '…as IEPs are such a crucial part of SEN intervention, this should be built into the job description of new teachers', while Carrie believed that IEPs needed a coordinator all to themselves….

Seven of the ten SENCOs felt 'reasonably happy' with the format of their IEPs, and considered that the refinements to them since their introduction made them easier to use and of more value to classroom teachers. Three SENCOs still believed that IEPs were far too complicated, and did not relate to what went on in the classroom. One suggested that attention to this point was going to be vital, in the light of the onset of Literacy and Numeracy Hours:

> IEPs don't serve any purpose at all if they fail to keep pace with new developments. As the Literacy Hour will definitely be used by [OFSTED] inspectors as a benchmark of quality, we have to make sure that the two things [Literacy Hour and IEP] are integrated. And that's going to be a lot of work for someone…me! (Max)

SEN Coordinators' views on the logistics of internal collaboration

All of the SENCOs indicated in conversation that the biggest barrier to their work was the unsatisfactory nature of internal collaboration. This term covers a multitude of highly sensitive areas, of course: lack of leadership from the head teacher, failure to receive the support of the senior management team, personality clashes resulting in a refusal to cooperate, time constraints and the need for appropriately focused staff development. What was significant in the study was that six of the SENCOs felt that internal, rather than external, collaboration required the most effort on their part.

All of the SENCOs highlighted leadership qualities and commitment to SEN as being the single most important factor in ensuring that the work of the SENCOs was effective. Lorna, for example, felt that the leadership of the head teacher was vital because 'I have been able to do things regarding SEN which haven't exactly been popular but which have been accepted because our head is dynamic and personable: everyone wants to please her because they respect her.' In contrast Anne was scathing about the cursory treatment that the Code and its implementation had received from her head teacher: 'Mr Farr is only interested in window-dressing. So providing everything looks fine for the parents and for any external people, then he's happy. But I have never had the feeling that he's committed to the work I do.'

In eight cases, SENCOs indicated that managing SEN within their school could be made difficult, sometimes impossible, without the support of all of their colleagues. Where this was forthcoming it created a situation in which '...everyone benefits, from pupils to teachers to helpers. As long as we keep the idea in our heads that if I fail to do something it means that somebody else might have to do it, then we'll be alright' (Josie). Of course, such positive relationships will not always be obtainable, as Carrie pointed out: 'I am sure that many SENCOs dread asking at least somebody on their staff to do some SEN-related task – I know I do. There is one teacher who feels that SEN matters have nothing whatsoever to do with her. I try to by-pass her as much as possible – we hardly speak.'

SEN Coordinators' views on inclusion

All of the SENCOs interviewed supported the principles underpinning the green paper *Excellence for All Children* (DfEE 1997c). Significantly, five SENCOs had established strong links with local special schools, although none of the partner schools were for children with perceived behaviour problems. All of the SENCOs believed that in most cases it was possible to include all learning disabilities within the mainstream; reserve was, however, expressed about the preparedness of many mainstream teachers to accommodate EBD pupils within their classrooms. All of the respondents believed that parents and children should be integrally involved in decision making concerning placement, and that inclusion should not be driven by the ideological wishes of professionals.

However, if full inclusion was to be made a practical reality, the SENCOs in this study felt that certain changes needed to be made to the way in which SEN provision within schools was managed. Top of their list of priorities was resourcing, including new infrastructures. Kim, for example, believed that '...the principle of inclusion is dead in the water if it is not backed up by a huge investment of money. Our school simply couldn't cope with the children from Copsea [local special school] without a major building programme. I'm afraid that they would attempt some half-baked scheme, and the children would definitely suffer then.'

Staff training was a major priority identified by these SENCOs. Max argued that 'We all think we know a lot about SEN. But in fact we have only skimmed the surface, and I think that mainstream staff need to be fully immersed in the philosophy of special schools as well. Why should their [special school] staff have to adapt to our way of working?' As Anne goes on to say, 'This means that the government is going to have to put its money where its mouth is.' Part of the need for staff development relates to attitudes, and, as Carrie warned, 'Given the way that one or two teachers and classroom assistants interact with even Stage 3 kids they need to be sent on a long course to change them – and even that might not work.'

SEN Coordinators' views on whole-school SEN policies

According to OFSTED, all the schools inspected '…had an SEN policy which complied broadly with the guidance contained in DfEE Circular 6/94' (OFSTED 1997:8). The SENCOs interviewed in this study were generally satisfied with the written document developed by their schools, but expressed some concern at gaps between the policy and what actually happens in practice. Kim described the process of constructing a revised version as '…policy-making by number. We knew that we were going to be OFSTEDed [sic] and so we just took the guidance document and made sure that we covered everything. In hindsight I know that everything was certainly not in place…'

Without exception, the SENCOs reported that the policy had been developed by the SENCO together with the senior management of the school, although four SENCOs expressly indicated that the initial discussion on the content of a revised policy was undertaken during a staff development session or staff meeting. Only in one instance was mention made of either parents or the children.

One of the important contributions of the kind of data provided above is to provide an indication of the complex nature of the SENCO's duties in managing SEN, and to place these within a personal and institutional context. Moreover, it confirms that, like IEPs and the Code of Practice itself, the work that SENCOs do should be kept under constant review. Equally, it illustrates the value of SENCOs interacting with each other, an approach whose value has been confirmed by many commentators. By such means can SENCOs appraise their own work and that of others, and incorporate good practice from elsewhere.

It is nice to be able to conclude with a reiteration of the positive feedback from Her Majesty's Chief Inspector as evidence of the work that SENCOs have done: 'Provision for pupils with special educational needs is good in six out of ten schools and rarely inadequate...Special needs coordinators have established appropriate procedures for keeping a register of pupils' special educational needs and for preparing and revising individual action plans' (OFSTED 1998a:26). For those familiar with the rationed positives of individual OFSTED reports, this constitutes almost stratospheric praise.

Chapter 5

The impact of LEA policy on the role of the SENCO

Roy Evans and Jim Docking

Introduction

The recent publication of *National Standards for Special Educational Needs Coordinators* (TTA 1998) provides a necessary reminder that the provision of effective support to all children who exhibit learning difficulties and have identified special educational needs is essentially a whole-school matter. By emphasising also the key outcomes of coordination, the *National Standards* document re-focuses attention on the professional educational or pedagogical challenges connected with identifying and meeting special educational needs whenever and however they occur. Recent evidence has tended to suggest that whilst the Education Act 1993 and subsequent Code of Practice were welcomed, in so far as they strengthened arrangements in support of entitlement, the professional issues which figured strongly in the discourse of Warnock have tended to become submerged by a widespread preoccupation with administrative procedures.

Ensuring that no child is prevented from accessing the full scope of the entitlement curriculum through failure to modify content and adapt teaching methods was a critical message replayed throughout the 1980s and culminating in the publication by the National Curriculum Council of 'A Curriculum for All' (Curriculum Guidance 2; NCC 1989). By emphasising the role that ordinary teachers could play in identifying and meeting the special educational needs of pupils' the *Guidance* effectively carried forward the view that good practice in teaching such pupils was no different from providing effective learning experiences for pupils generally. Much of the rhetoric prior to 1993 was concerned with mechanisms for sharing expertise, for demystifying special education practice and for enskilling ordinary class and subject teachers to 'own' the professional issues by enabling them to acquire enlarged repertoires of pedagogical strategies. All this through working with a 'special needs teacher' who possessed shareable knowledge and skills and the time and disposition to make them available.

However, the thrust of the statutory orders and non-statutory guidance that have flowed into schools over the past decade has had the effect of giving a sterile presentation of what schools should do. Whilst the effects on curriculum organisation have been substantial, the effects also on the coordination of provision for special educational needs have been profound, and with them the way in which tasks have become conceptualised and roles and relationships defined. The Code seems to be based on the assumption that 'tightening the screws' rather than changing practices would make things better (Dyer 1995), and has been criticised for concentrating unduly on matters relating to identification and assessment while teachers lack sufficient guidance on effective strategies (Garner 1995). At the same time, the system for training teachers in SEN remains threadbare and fragmented, and does not necessarily result in improved practice in the classroom (SENTC 1996). OFSTED have yet to undertake a specific review of the way higher education institutes (HEIs) provide for SEN within programmes of initial teacher training, a matter of crucial significance to the way in which entrants to the profession think about their responsibilities and can evidence competence in designing and employing appropriate learning tasks and managing the learning environment.

Meanwhile, the matter is compounded as LEAs, in adapting to the culture of commodification in education, are in danger of leaving responsibility for pupils with special needs (particularly those without statements) to schools alone (Vincent *et al.* 1994), and without effective systems to hold schools accountable for their work with SEN children (Audit Commission 1994). However, in this latter regard there is the additional complicating factor that LEA 'policy' on SEN is not always reflected in the financial allocation mechanisms employed to resource the work in schools, whilst schools themselves have, as yet, poorly articulated and ill-defined procedures for targeting resources, tracking their deployment and monitoring their effectiveness. To a degree, schools find the issue of 'effectiveness' an intractable problem to solve, owing partly to the subjectivity involved in judgements over children's learning and behaviour and partly to the lack of hard-edged criteria by which added value may be assessed.

The SENCO's role, and their experience of working within evolving frameworks driven by the Code, cannot be divorced from LEA policy or leadership. Neither can such experiences be considered as anything other than deeply influenced by the particular character of each individual work place, its ethos, vision and quality of management and responsiveness to change. We may agree with Dyson (1991:57) when he argues that

> If there are teachers who are charged with some sort of responsibility for children with special needs then their primary role is, logically, not to provide additional resources or carry out special teaching but to promote the process of curricular reconstruction

and to view the SENCO's role as manifestly an 'influential' one. We may even agree that within such a concept of 'role', responsibility for initiating and supporting transformations in colleagues thinking about the curriculum would figure strongly. But to agree with the logic requires one to have made a choice of a model of support, which comes close to what Hart (1991) described as the whole-curriculum model. To implement such a model requires the special needs person (coordinator) to be a resource to colleagues within the framework of a clearly understood policy on special needs which transcends the purely procedural aspects of provision and encodes 'practice' within the overarching model of curriculum delivery. However, as we have noted elsewhere, (see e.g. Evans *et al.* 1995), one of the major issues facing schools that we have researched is the lack in many of any clear sense of the pedagogical and curricular relatedness of SEN policy to broader issues of curriculum philosophy and the organisation of teaching. SEN policy is still, for many schools, a matter of providing individualised support – from which perspective it remains essentially conflicted, characterised by pragmatism and expediency in the deployment of resources, and notably at secondary level driven by the professional judgement of the SENCO. As the tight grip of LEA advisory services on policy directions in schools has loosened in the wake of LMS (local management of schools), cultures of special needs support vary markedly from one school to another even within a single LEA. The 'lived world' of the SENCO is now, more than for decades, constructed through competition for scarce resources both within and between schools. Such issues influence not only how SENCOs see their role, but also how they experience it. Part of this chapter briefly explores issues relating to funding in so far as they influence perceptions of the available resource.

Comparisons between LEAs in matters concerning provision and its funding are generally regarded as being notoriously difficult. Within the SEN field the difficulties are due to differences in: the priorities and policies of individual LEAs in response to government funding and local circumstances; the nature of the LMS formula and the LMSS (local management of special schools) formula and the lack of any uniformity of practice in the use of proxy indicators to set non-statemented support; the possible inclusion of additional factors, for example of a social nature as a means of targeting funding for SEN; the level of historic and existing provision in both mainstream and special schools within an LEA; accounting practices within the LEAs and schools themselves; the nature and degree of centrally retained funding; the availability and cost to schools of service level agreements; the extent of parental lobbying.

There are particular operational difficulties in comparing SEN provision across LEAs and funding. This is due in part to the relativity of the concept of SEN and a persistent lack of clarity about the nature of the pupils to whom the 1981 Act is intended to apply. In part it is due also to differences in the decision-making processes in the LEA which lead to the assessment of SEN and possible statementing. To consider the role of the SENCO in isolation from key formative influences which set the ideological and practical parameters in action is to miss an important opportunity for understanding the richness and diversity of experience across schools. This having been said, the purpose of the present chapter is to provide a contemporary research-based view of how SEN Coordinators in primary and secondary schools view their role, what issues may be identified as impeding progress towards policy realisation, and the tensions that remain unresolved, against a background of issues connected with funding, policy, and management. To this end, the evidence collected through an extensive programme of research in five LEAs will be used to:

- provide a comparative analysis of placement practice and the mechanisms and levels of resourcing statemented and non-statemented pupils aged 5 to 16;
- provide an analysis of the factors which would need to be taken into account in implementing a policy of increased placement of statemented pupils in mainstream schools.

The research survey

The research was undertaken with the collaboration of four London boroughs and an adjacent county authority. The following data sources were available:

- LEA documentation including policy statements, LMS and LMSS schemes, audit reports, Section 42 statements, and local guidance to schools as well as the public at large.

- A questionnaire survey of all SENCOs in all primary and secondary schools in the five LEAs. Amongst the matters respondents were asked to comment on were: staffing resources; issues relating to the implementation of the Code; the level of priority they would assign to aspects of SEN provision which might be in need of improvement; factors that might be disincentives to a policy of increased inclusivity. The response rate to the questionnaire was 70 per cent (72 per cent primary and 62 per cent secondary). This generated returns from 437 schools; 373 primary phase and 64 secondary. Primary phase responses included the full range of school types.
- Focussed interviews with a sample of heads, SENCOs, teachers and governors across all five authorities, including mainstream schools, special schools and mainstream schools with attached units or special resource provision.
- Interviews with LEA officers responsible for financial operations.

Provision

Across the five LEAs considerable variations were found in provision for SEN. As can be seen from Table 5.1, rates of statementing, for example, differed by over 1 per cent, the proportions of statemented pupils placed in both mainstream and special schools by almost 20 per cent, and the proportion of pupils placed outside the LEA by over 7 per cent. No doubt these variations are in part a reflection of the varying size and demographic features of the LEAs, and the figures may also vary somewhat in relation to the numbers of pupils attending fee-paying schools or who are educated otherwise than at school.

Among the questionnaire returns, the average proportion of pupils with SEN in mainstream school was 3.7 per cent statemented and 17.2 per cent non-statemented (Stages 1 to 4 of the Code). However, as Table 5.2 reveals, there were marked differences between authorities at each age-phase. This was particularly so at secondary level, where the percentages between authorities varied by as much as 11.6 per cent in the case of statemented pupils and 19.6 per cent for SEN pupils without statements.

Our point here is that such variations, as well as those considered below, will influence the nature of the tasks that SENCOs undertake, and, alongside other factors, the effectiveness with which the desired outcomes to coordination may be achieved.

Funding

Budgetary practices also varied. The lowest-spending LEA allocated 10.3 per cent of its General School Budget (GSB) to account for all special needs other than out-borough placements: the highest-spending LEA allocated 17.2 per cent of GSB, a difference of 7 per cent.

Table 5.1 Provision for special educational needs

Range of provision across 5 LEAs (%)			
	Lowest	Highest	Difference
Rates of statementing	2.7	3.8	1.1
Proportion of statemented pupils in mainstream schools and units	45.0	64.0	19.0
Proportion of statemented pupils in special schools (incl. out-LEA)	36.0	55.0	19.0
Out-LEA special school placements	7.8	15.0	7.2
Special school places as proportion of total school population	0.9	1.6	0.7

Source: Section 42 statements for 1995/96 plus advice from LEA officers.

Table 5.2 Pupils with SEN in mainstream schools

Percentage of school roll				
	Statemented pupils		Non-statemented pupils	
	All auths.	Lowest–highest	All auths.	Lowest–highest
Infant/first	5.0	1.9 – 5.3	15.8	13.9–24.6
Junior/middle	2.6	1.9 – 2.8	22.8	18.4–33.4
All-through primary	3.0	1.8 – 5.5	17.5	14.2–21.6
Secondary	4.2	2.0 – 13.6	13.2	9.8–29.4
All schools	3.7	2.4 – 4.4	17.2	14.9–22.6

Non-statemented pupils

All the LEAs assessed schools' resource needs for non-statemented pupils through the use of proxy factors. In all but one LEA, these included free school meals; but other indicators such as reading scores, SAT scores and school audits on provided criteria were also employed. The average per capita support for primary pupils ranged from £63.02, or 3.7 per cent of the Aggregated Schools Budget (ASB), to £22.53, or 1.3 per cent; for secondary pupils, support ranged from £70.05, or 3.3 per cent of the ASB, to £22.81 or 1.0 per cent. However, there was no consistent sense in which the funds distributed favoured either primary or secondary pupils: in three authorities it was higher at secondary level, though in one case the difference was marginal, and in two it was higher at primary.

Of course, these figures represent only a small fraction of the delegated resources that schools use to support non-statemented special needs. Each of the LEAs emphasised that special needs in Stages 1 to 3 of the Code of Practice were funded principally through the age-weighted pupil unit (AWPU). In order to interpret the possible significance of the AWPU and the add-on resources distributed via SEN proxy indicators, we calculated the percentage contributions to the Aggregated Schools Budget (ASB) and the Potential Schools Budget (PSB) via the AWPU, using Year 5 as a marker for the primary phase and Year 8 for secondary. We found that whilst the AWPU (primary) differed by an average of £134 per pupil between the highest and lowest figures among the authorities and the AWPU (secondary) by £452, the variations were considerably attenuated through the differential effects of different formula elements. Consequently, when the ASB was itself used to calculate average pupil budget shares, the difference of £134 at primary level was reduced to £34 for the same two authorities, and the difference of £452 at secondary level was reduced to £161 for the same two authorities. Thus, for those particular authorities, the apparent generosity of one over the other became markedly reduced. At the same time, among all the five LEAs, the identification of the most and least generous authorities changed at both primary and secondary levels, though the gap was now reduced to £121 instead of £134 for primary pupils and £252 instead of £452 for secondary.

It is worth noting that in no LEA was there a weighting factor for concentration of SEN in particular schools, nor was there any recognition of the added costs of administration in schools with large numbers of children at Stages 1 to 3 of the Code.

Statemented pupils

In another set of calculations, we could find no strong or consistent relationship between funding arrangements and statementing practices. In our comparisons of two authorities which were demographically and economically comparable and had similar statementing rates, SEN expenditure in one ran at 14 per cent of the GSB but at only 10.7 per cent in the other. There seemed to be no explanation for these differences other than those embedded within the customs and practices of the LEAs. Another two authorities which were the most socially and economically advantaged had very different statementing rates (2.7 and 3.75 per cent), yet similar levels of support at both primary and secondary levels. We conclude from these comparisons that the failure of schools to cope with SEN within the available resources is not simply explained by either the level of resourcing or the socio-economic context. Part of the problem is the definition of SEN itself and the differing ways in which LEAs perceive the purposes of statementing and manage the pressures which drive it.

The pupil-led funding allocations for special schools was on the basis of 'banding', but the number of bands to which pupils were allocated varied from five in one authority to 19 in another. Comparisons are difficult, however, since there was no common terminology, and band descriptors and the weightings attached to bands varied between authorities. Variation was again apparent in the method of allocating funds to special units attached to mainstream schools. According to authority, these units were funded principally either through a combination of place factor and pupil factor by formula, or through pupil-led resources alone.

Not one of the five LEAs was able to accommodate the placement needs of all its statemented children. All therefore supplemented provision in out-authority placement, though in one LEA this was very low. Elsewhere, the average placement costs varied from £9,978 to £23,377 per pupil per year.

Monitoring the effectiveness of funding

Although all the LEA documents recognised the monitoring of funds as the authority's responsibility, none of the LEAs took responsibility for monitoring non-statemented funding. Some produced guidelines, but practices appeared to differ greatly both between and within authorities. No specific requirement had been placed upon governors, whose comments during interviews revealed how ill-equipped they were to judge the effectiveness of the use of resources. Invariably, governing bodies subscribed to an act-of-faith syndrome, relying on the views of the head or SENCO, and no governing body systematically required reports on the effectiveness of the school's support strategies. In contrast, accountability for the use of funds for statemented pupils was much more in evidence and had greater LEA involvement.

SEN policy and management

In all LEAs, SEN policy was shaped by professional groups, each of which seemed to enjoy a high level of autonomy. In decision-making, there was little evidence of cross-team reporting or working or the full involvement of other agencies, such as the health service.

All LEAs had a commitment to staff development. However, few defined which staff, and the major areas where mainstream schools felt support was needed was provided for in different ways across the authorities. This appeared to be a direct consequence of delegation of funds to schools, removing from LEAs the power to ensure that effective use was made of these in terms of generally agreed priorities. We found no evidence of LEAs drawing upon the expertise of special school teachers for mainstream staff development. Much of the training seemed to focus on the procedural and administrative details of the system rather than on the effectiveness of different approaches to learning and teaching.

Status and role of SENCOs

From questionnaire responses, the average fraction of non-contact time which SENCOs were allowed for coordinating special needs was greater in secondary than primary schools (0.30 $v.$ 0.15), though here again the figures differed widely between authorities. Spearman rank correlations showed weak and generally insignificant associations between numbers of pupils with SEN (statemented or non-statemented) on the one hand, and SENCOs' non-contact time on the other.

SENCOs were asked to describe their personal situation by responding Yes/No to a range of indicators. The results are presented in Table 5.3. In virtually all cases, differences between authorities did not reach statistical significance. This was also the case with respect to age-phase differences on certain matters. Across primary and secondary schools, the great majority of SENCOs were permanent members of staff (93 per cent) and had had training in the Code of Practice (90 per cent), while two-thirds claimed that they liaised with all relevant staff at least weekly even though around half were also class or subject teachers. Of the 85 per cent with job descriptions, 94 per cent could make decisions regarding material resources for special needs, though only one-third could do so for NNEB staff.

Table 5.3 The role and status of SENCOs.

| | Percentage of SENCOs responding 'Yes' | | | | | |
| | Primary (N=369) | | Secondary (N=63) | | Differences between primary and secondary | |
Role/status of SENCO	All auths.	Least–Most	All auths.	Least–Most	Chi-square	p
Is a permanent member of staff	92	82–100	98	97–100	2.23	NS
Has a full-time contract	79	52–100	95	91–100	8.39	0.01
Has a job description	84	73–92	95	83–100	7.70	0.05
Of those with job description, responsibilities include:						
• making decisions re staff development	76	68–87	81	67–100	9.50	0.01
• making decisions re support staff	60	38–64	90	67–100	17.97	0.001
• making decisions re classroom assistants	58	38–67	91	63–100	20.37	0.001
• making decisions re NNEB staff	31	12–36	36	0–60	0.06	NS
• making decisions re material resources	90	88–95	98	89–100	2.66	NS
Is also a class/subject teacher	48	44–66	55	17–67	0.59	NS
Has also other coordinating responsibilities	69	41–84	37	17–56	24.49	0.001
Is a member of the school's senior team	61	58–76	22	0–67	31.38	0.001
Has had training in Code of Practice	91	81-96	84	60–100	2.26	NS
Has qualification in SEN	30	7–40	65	50–100	27.93	0.001
Is allocated specific time for SEN teaching	43	24–62	67	50–100	13.80	0.001
Spends more time supporting children than staff	63	49–68	90	50–93	17.92	0.001
Liaises with all relevant staff at least weekly	64	56–81	74	5–100	2.25	NS
The way professional time is spent has been significantly changed by Code	67	58–86	83	56–100	5.42	0.05

On other matters there were marked age-phase differences. In spite of generally high percentages, SENCOs in secondary schools were significantly more likely than their primary colleagues to be on a full-time contract (95 *v.* 79 per cent), to have a job description (95 *v.* 84 per cent), to have a qualification in SEN (65 *v.* 30 per cent), to be allocated time specifically for teaching pupils with SEN (67 *v.* 43 per cent), to spend more time supporting children than staff (90 *v.* 63 per cent), and to feel that their use of professional time had been markedly changed by the Code of Practice (83 *v.* 67 per cent). Secondary SENCOs with job descriptions were also significantly more likely to have the authority to make decisions about support teaching staff (90 *v.* 60 per cent), classroom assistants (91 *v.* 58 per cent), and staff development (81 *v.* 76 per cent). Primary SENCOs, on the other hand, were significantly more likely to be members of their school's senior management team (61 *v.* 22 per cent), though significantly more also had other coordinating responsibilities (69 *v.* 37 per cent).

The Code of Practice and its impact

SENCOs were invited in the questionnaire to express their views on a range of issues using a four-point scale from 'strongly agree' to 'strongly disagree'. The results are shown in Tables 5.4 to 5.6. Although there was a range of perceptions depending on the authority, the significant differences between mean ratings were all between primary and secondary age-phases.

From Table 5.4, it can be seen that secondary SENCOs were significantly less likely than their primary colleagues to welcome the early involvement of parents, though levels of agreement on this matter were very high across the age-phases (88 per cent secondary, 98 per cent primary). Markedly greater age-phase contrast emerged on whether colleagues understood their responsibilities with respect to Stages 1 to 3 of the Code, only 41 per cent secondary *v.* 73 per cent primary giving a positive response.

In both primary and secondary schools, widespread concern was expressed regarding the amount of time needed to meet the Code's requirements. But this was all the more conspicuous among secondary SENCOs, who were significantly less inclined than their primary colleagues to accept that the paperwork associated with the Code was a valuable use of teachers' time (13 *v.* 28 per cent), to agree that they had time to liaise with other staff in the writing of IEPs (19 *v.* 28 per cent), to recognise such collaboration as a valuable use of their time (12 *v.* 41 per cent), or to believe that teachers had time to liaise among themselves

Table 5.4 SENCOs' views on the Code and its impact

			Percentage of responses[1]				Mean rating	SD	t value[2]	df	p
		N	Str agree	Agree	Disagree	Str agree					
Teachers understand their responsibilities with regard to Stages 1, 2 and 3 of the Code	Pri	372	17	55	23	5	1.85	0.76	5.99	80.92	0.000
	Sec	63	2	40	35	24	1.19	0.82			
Teachers believe extra resources will be needed to give proper regard to the Code	Pri	372	72	19	6	2	2.61	0.72	1.23	107.98	NS
	Sec	64	73	23	3	0	2.70	0.53			
The early involvement of parents is welcomed	Pri	364	79	19	2	0	2.77	0.46	2.53	70.63	0.01
	Sec	64	67	20	9	3	2.52	0.80			
The Code is changing the way SENs are assessed and monitored	Pri	364	48	38	11	2	2.32	0.77	0.68	426	NS
	Sec	64	47	33	19	2	2.52	0.82			
The Code will mean fewer children are referred to an LEA for formal assessment	Pri	365	34	32	24	10	1.90	0.98	1.13	426	NS
	Sec	63	41	30	21	8	2.05	0.97			
Teachers are confident of their ability to cater for most SENs with appropriate support	Pri	370	10	34	4	10	1.35	0.89	0.82	430	NS
	Sec	62	11	37	37	15	1.45	0.88			
Teachers have time to liaise in respect of the IEPs where necessary	Pri	373	7	17	17	48	0.83	0.96	4.59	105.18	0.000
	Sec	63	3	21	21	73	0.37	0.70			
The SENCO has time to liaise in the writing of IEPs	Pri	368	10	37	37	35	1.02	0.96	2.51	430	0.01
	Sec	64	.3	30	30	52	0.70	0.85			
The paperwork associated with the Code is a valuable use of teachers' time	Pri	369	3	44	44	27	1.04	0.80	3.28	430	0.001
	Sec	63	2	41	41	46	0.68	0.74			
Teachers find collaborating with the writing and reviewing of IEPs to be an effective use of their time	Pri	367	5	43	43	16	1.30	0.79	5.57	425	0.000
	Sec	60	0	47	47	42	0.70	0.67			

N = number of respondents for the item

Means are based on the range 3 (strongly agree) to 0 (strongly disagree)

1: Some percentages do not total 100 because of rounding

2: t values were calculated using SPSS on the basis or unequal variances, as estimated by Levene's Test for Equality of Variance

about the writing of IEPs (6 *v.* 35 per cent). During the interviews with school staff, the overwhelming burden of paperwork came through loud and clear in every case. One SENCO complained that there was so much to do at Stage 1 that teachers were wary about initiating the processes, suggesting that the Code's bureaucracy could make it counterproductive and delay support for children in need.

On four matters related to the Code, however, no significant age-phase differences emerged from responses to the questionnaire. First, overwhelmingly (92 per cent) SENCOs took the view that extra resources were needed to implement the Code properly, almost three-quarters registering 'strong' agreement with this item. During the interviews, SENCOs and heads in all LEAs spoke of resources from the school budget as a whole being used to ensure adequate provision for non-statemented pupils, and in two LEAs this comment was also made with respect to statemented pupils. One source of the problem was turbulence in school rolls which had not been accounted for in the previous budget. As one secondary head explained, 'It's a needs-led budget demand and that way you can't make an accurate prediction.' In any case, targeting of resources was regarded as formulaic, and, as another head said, such formulae as are used do not cater for the idiosyncrasies of individual need. There was also general concern that the new triggering mechanisms being adopted by the LEAs would reduce funding still further as the move towards harder-edged criteria pushed ahead.

The other matters on which secondary and primary teachers concurred in their questionnaire responses concerned assessment procedures and staff competence. The vast majority of SENCOs (86 per cent) agreed that the Code was changing the way special needs were assessed and monitored, while around two-thirds thought that the Code would mean fewer children referred to the LEA for assessment. Perhaps the most alarming revelation was that fewer than half of all SENCOs (43 per cent) believed that teachers were confident in their ability to cater for most special needs, even with appropriate support.

Levels and models of support

As Table 5.5 shows, almost 60 per cent of SENCOs believed teachers to be satisfied that existing support for statemented children ensured appropriate access to the curriculum, but only about half expressed satisfaction with the deployment of existing support for non-statemented pupils, the percentage being significantly less in secondary (44 per cent) than primary schools (51 per cent) . More than two-thirds in both primary

Table 5.5 SENCOs' views on existing levels of support

		Percentage of responses[1]				Mean rating	SD	t value[2]	df	p
	N	Str agree	Agree	Disagree	Str agree					
Teachers are satisfied with the the deployment of existing support for non-statemented children	Pri	370	6	39	38	17	1.35	0.83	3.23	430	0.001
	Sec	62	0	32	34	34	0.98	0.82			
Teachers are satisfied that existing support for statemented children ensures appropriate curriculum access	Pri	359	14	46	12	12	1.61	0.87	0.68	421	NS
	Sec	64	14	41	16	16	1.53	0.93			
Parents are a source of pressure for additional resources to support learning	Pri	362	31	37	5	5	1.94	0.89	0.71	421	NS
	Sec	61	25	43	7	7	1.85	0.87			

N = number of respondents for the item

Means are based on the range 3 (strongly agree) to O (strongly disagree)

1: Some percentages do not total 100 because of rounding

2: t values were calculated using SPSS on the basis or unequal variances, as estimated by Levene's Test for Equality of Variance

and secondary schools agreed that parents were a source of pressure for additional resources to support learning.

During interviews with school staff about support issues, those in secondary schools again emerged as the more concerned. The perception was that the language of the Code was primary in its orientation, and that its implication for secondary schools had not been thought through. In primary schools, most teachers worked in close liaison with the SENCO, had plenty of opportunity for discussion, and felt that their opinions were taken into account in policy and resourcing matters. Even though they often felt that more help in the classroom was needed, they took it for granted that it was their responsibility to provide differentiated learning for all pupils. In secondary schools, however, where children were taught by subject specialists, subject staff lacked methods of curriculum support, and there were understandable problems of consultation, coordination, and targeting resources effectively.

The difficulties clustered around four broad issues:

1 *Allocating support to children.* Because resources were so ill-matched to need, schools found difficulty in arriving at appropriate criteria for targeting the support available. One school's solution, whereby a child with SEN received 0.1 of a support teacher regardless of his or her needs, seemed numerically but not educationally equitable; another school concentrated on Year 7 children at the expense of other years (which 'get help but it is very hit and miss...it is an impossible task to spread it so thinly'). Commonly, the focus was on support in English and mathematics, which in some cases meant children being withdrawn from other subjects to receive extra support in these core areas.

2 *Quality of support.* Many teachers regretted the lack of sustained support. 'The biggest thing I would like to do is to ensure that I saw all the kids that I teach for a short time every day'. The other concern was lack of specialist support: 'They're not always subject-literate... he's explained something to the kids [who look] blank because they can't understand his terminology.' There was also the problem of obtaining specialist materials, which were much more easily available for English and mathematics than for other subjects.

3 *Negotiation between subject teacher and support teacher.* Numerous comments revealed the need for greater liaison and a more collaborative model of working with support teachers.

4 *The 'start from search' philosophy.* The benefits of record-keeping were frequently jeopardised when children's records from their previous school were disregarded. This practice, which was particularly marked in two authorities, seemed to deny a recognition

of a child's persistent learning difficulty. At the same time, some children with no records were found to have greater support needs than those with records, while some teachers complained about the slowness in the arrival of records from the previous school or the 'waste of time' preparing evidence when pupils subsequently left.

Statementing

Both the questionnaire and the interviews brought out concern about the quality of statementing. From the questionnaire responses, as Table 5.6 shows, perceptions of the quality of guidance in statements varied significantly between age-phases. Although over half of primary SENCOs (56 per cent) believed that teachers found statements useful as a basis for planning learning experiences, little over a quarter (27 per cent) did so in secondary schools. Differences between authorities were also evident here, with percentages varying from 30 to 62 per cent. About a quarter of all SENCOs believed that statementing was viewed mainly as a means of securing extra resources for the school as a whole.

The interviews suggested that, in general, schools were left insufficiently involved in the statementing process. Staff were concerned about the opacity of some statements which, while seen as recently improving in quality, were still often imprecise and rather unhelpful. Nor was it always clear why the LEA had decided to maintain, or not maintain, a statement. Part of the explanation may lie in the degree to which parental influence impinged upon schools and the LEAs. Whereas school staff and governors did not pick up parental pressure as an important concern from their perspective, LEA officers suggested that this was a high priority as far as they were concerned, as was the power and influence of educational psychologists and the way funding was allocated. Some LEAs saw increased centralisation of decision making as creating a better basis for control in dealing with parental and professional pressures for statementing and placement decisions.

Integration

On the subject of integration (Table 5.6), as many as 71 per cent of SENCOs overall indicated in their questionnaire responses that staff were sympathetic to the principle of integrating statemented pupils. Although there were no marked age-phase differences, the percentages varied between 60 and 90 per cent according to authority. However, about 40 per cent of primary and secondary SENCOs believed that some teachers were

Table 5.6 SENCOs' views on the Code and its impact

		Percentage of responses[1]				Mean rating	SD	t value[2]	df	p
	N	Str agree	Agree	Disagree	Str agree					
Statementing is viewed mainly as a means of securing resources for the school	Pri	369	10	18	37	35	1.22	1.08	1.68	429	NS
	Sec	62	3	16	30	52	1.47	1.16			
Teachers find statements useful as the basis for planning learning experiences for children	Pri	368	18	39	33	11	1.63	0.90	5.18	92.73	0.000
	Sec	63	3	24	49	23	1.06	0.78			
Teachers are sympathetic to the principle of integrating statemented pupils	Pri	370	18	51	24	7	1.81	0.81	1.86	429	NS
	Sec	61	26	51	21	2	2.02	0.74			
Teachers are the major source of pressure for segregated special provision	Pri	363	12	29	36	23	1.30	0.95	1.43	421	NS
	Sec	60	8	25	37	30	1.12	0.94			

N = number of respondents for the item

Means are based on the range 3 (strongly agree) to O (strongly disagree)

1: Some percentages do not total 100 because of rounding

2: t values were calculated using SPSS on the basis or unequal variances, as estimated by Levene's Test for Equality of Variance

a major source of pressure for segregated provision, though here again the proportion varied between authorities (from 29 to 59 per cent).

When SENCOs were asked to indicate the disincentives to accommodating additional statemented pupils, easily the main factor from a list of six was 'existing levels of resourcing' (ranked first in all authorities). This was followed by 'the reservations of colleagues in the light of other colleagues'. The other factors – 'availability of physical space', the 'balance of pupils within the school', 'parents' reservations', and 'governors' concerns about school performance' (the latter ranked sixth in all authorities) – seemed to be less of a problem overall.

In all authorities, however, SENCOs agreed that their views on integration were heavily dependent on the nature of the child's needs. The ubiquitous concern was regarding children with EBD (especially in secondary schools) and severe learning difficulties. Our interviews with school staff and governors confirmed these perceptions. Teachers were particularly concerned at the prospect of accepting more statemented children with emotional and behavioural problems if class size was not reduced and/or they were not given more teaching support staff. Only one LEA, and then at primary level only, organised specifically designated help in this area through an advisory team.

Priorities for improvement

In the questionnaire, SENCOs were invited to indicate their preferences from a choice of nine aspects of SEN provision where improvement could be needed. The two factors that emerged as top priorities were, first, increased financial support for non-statemented pupils and, secondly, more timetabled opportunities for liaison and planning. The two areas of least concern were relationships with parents and the attitudes of colleagues towards children with SEN. The support given to improving access to external support services and providing greater opportunities to obtain qualifications and training was more varied, but quite high in some quarters.

Discussion

Our data showed considerable variations across the five authorities regarding rates of statementing, the proportion of statemented pupils in mainstream schools and funding arrangements for SEN, though average pupil budget shares were found to differ less when all formula elements were introduced into the calculations. Levels of funding and rates of statementing did not seem strongly or consistently related, even when the socio-economic context was taken into account. Although LEAs were heavily involved in monitoring the use of funds for statemented pupils, none took such responsibility in relation to non-statemented pupils with SEN, and school governors lacked the criteria and information by which they could judge if resources were being used effectively. In all LEAs, SEN policy was determined largely by professional groups, with little evidence of cross-team work or the involvement of other agencies, while staff development was concerned mainly with procedure and administration rather than the effectiveness of different strategies.

Governors, heads, SENCOs, teachers and LEA officials alike viewed the Code of Practice as being potentially useful. All the same, our findings from the questionnaire to SENCOs and our interviews with school staff and governors revealed a series of widespread concerns. Compared with their primary colleagues, secondary staff had been the more affected by the Code. They felt more strongly that their time was now spent less profitably, and they were more likely to criticise the levels and quality of arrangements for supporting children with SEN and the usefulness of statements in curriculum planning. Regardless of age-phase, however, schools believed that a proper implementation of the Code was dependent upon an injection of extra resources and the allocation of more time for planning and liaison. At the same time staff betrayed a widespread lack of confidence in their ability to cater for most special needs, even with support, and their sympathy with the principle of greater mainstreaming was tempered by their concern at the prospect of having to deal with more emotional and behaviour problems, for which the LEAs were seen to give inadequate support.

Our conclusions relate largely to LEA management practices and the need to establish a more effective partnership between schools and local authorities. We believe that authorities should provide an important enabling function and not simply a facilitating mechanism. In line with Bines and Thomas (1994), our view is that LEAs need to move away from their essentially bureaucratic ways of working and 'towards a model based on advocacy, which fosters inclusion, looks to the rights of the child and promotes cooperation amongst schools to meet SEN' (p. 61).

Given our findings that the effectiveness for provision of non-statemented children is weakly and ineffectively monitored, LEAs could help schools to identify the use to which SEN funding is put and require schools to set up a database of school development plans which have financial amounts set against priorities. School management and governing bodies would benefit by greater guidance in areas relating to cost-effectiveness, the targeting of resources, and an understanding of performance indicators for the effective use of resources and for the entry of pupils into Stage 4 of the Code. In view of the restricted time available to staff, LEAs could also provide more guidance for schools on how to manage the Code's paperwork, and they could include a weighting factor for support in favour of schools where there is a concentration of SEN pupils. LEAs should also ensure there is a common understanding about the definition of each stage in the Code, especially Stage 1, and that staff – particularly in secondary schools – understand their responsibilities under the Code.

As regards statementing practices, our findings suggest that LEAs need not only to remove the perceived unnecessary bureaucracy which delays statementing, but also to ensure that the rationale for decisions about statementing is consistent and effectively communicated to schools. Furthermore, statements need to be made more useful to schools by making explicit the child's curricular needs. The 'start from scratch' problem in transfer from school to school should also be addressed to maximise continuity and reduce unnecessary delay in ensuring the provision of needed support.

Equally, we believe that some of the current difficulties in funding SEN could be ameliorated if partner authorities established task groups to take earlier preventive action. Such groups could share experience of techniques for early identification of children who may require additional support in mainstream schools and collaborate in developing sharper and more child-centred approaches to identifying learning difficulties. They could also collaborate in developing models of resource allocation through individual risk assessment, clarify protocols for monitoring the effectiveness of support strategies, explore the difficulties in establishing a common view about the circumstances under which children enter Stage 4 of the Code, and encourage clusters of schools to share resources and expertise. Within such clusters, staff development forums could be established to draw upon the expertise of special schools and create more opportunities for teachers to obtain qualifications in special needs through routes such as accreditation of their own practice. Funding, however, needs to drive projects such as agreed performance indicators for pupil matching with different stages of the Code and resource-sharing of staff and materials.

Crucially, our evidence points to the need for more widespread opportunities for both teaching and support staff to receive training and qualifications to improve staff confidence in support strategies. Such action would clearly be advantageous given that (a) the cost of maintaining a statemented child in a mainstream school is a fraction of that involved in a special school placement, (b) staff are sympathetic to greater integration in principle, but (c) they lack confidence in dealing with special needs. Although steps are needed to improve access to external agencies and specialist support, our evidence suggests that there would be particular merit in LEAs taking initiatives in respect of pupils with EBD and specific learning difficulties, with the aim of spreading expertise around the schools.

Whatever the precise mechanisms, it is clear from our evidence that better structures are needed to raise levels of proficiency and confidence. We are at one with the central recommendation by the SENTC working party (1996), that since all teaching staff are involved with pupils with special education needs, 'a systematic plan of staff development must reach all teachers' (para 5:2).

Chapter 6

The early years: Luke's story

Sue Rice

When Luke started nursery school in the autumn term aged 3 years 4 months, it would have been all too easy to focus upon the more negative aspects of his behaviour. He rushed into the room and from one area to another without any apparent awareness of the trail of destruction he was leaving behind him. His activity had a frantic quality. He frequently snatched things from other children, knocked things over or emptied boxes. He loved water, but created abundant floods. He would roll around on the floor and underneath tables, and any attempt to include him in group situations were disastrous. He made little attempts to monitor his own bodily needs – apart from pointing to his trousers to indicate when they were wet. Noises, grunts and gestures accompanied this frenzy of activity.

Tina Bruce (1997) articulates ten principles which can be drawn from the long and distinguished tradition of early childhood education in this country. All of these underpin and support our school's practice when addressing the needs of young children, but the seventh in the list is especially pertinent in this context:

> What children can do (rather than what they cannot do) is the starting point of a child's education. (Bruce 1997:17)

Our first task then, if we were to support Luke's needs in the nursery, was to identify those things he could do and to discover the understanding he brought with him.

Margy Whalley (1997) emphasises the importance of knowing each child as an individual, and of recognising what they are able to do. She asserts that each of us have special needs, of one kind or another, and will need help at some time in our lives. It is interesting to ponder the idea that if we believe in inclusivity wherever possible (as the Code of Practice states) then there is no such thing as 'special educational needs', but just children with a variety of needs, some of whom will require a more sensitive and individual treatment.

In our school, a narrative style of observation, (Bartholomew and Bruce 1993) is a central tool in our identification of children's needs and interests, and in the collection of evidence for each child's profile. Careful observation of Luke was crucial in order to work with, rather than against, his preferred activity – we needed to find out what made him 'tick' (Bruce 1994). We also had to work closely with his parents because we wanted to learn from each other.

By the time Luke entered school he, and his family, had already been involved with other support agencies, particularly the speech therapist. There were concerns about the delays in other aspects of his development. The main focus was his lack of verbal communication, but his levels of functioning indicated a global delay. Very soon we met to devise an Individual Education Plan (IEP) for Luke and asked for an assessment by the educational psychologist. On her visit, she expressed concern about his ability to develop conceptual understanding and suggested that we should be assessing this through the provision of particular adult-directed tasks; perhaps, for example, sitting him down to make bead patterns. To someone who believes that young children should be actively involved in their learning, encouraged to make choices, to explore and investigate their environment and to operate autonomously rather than being directed by adults or learning 'skills' for the sake of them, this suggested approach posed a problem!

As part of a Master of Education degree (MEd), I undertook a research project, which considered how an awareness of the patterns in children's behaviour could be used to support their learning. In this, I drew on work begun at the Froebel Institute, Roehampton, by Chris Athey when she sought to find, describe and document common strands in the learning behaviour of young children. Athey, building upon the work of Piaget, sought to offer more positive descriptions of young children's learning. She showed how children draw upon the opportunities and experiences available, fitting them into their current behaviour pattern or 'schema'. She defines schema as 'a pattern of repeatable behaviour into which experiences are associated and that are gradually coordinated. Coordinators lead to higher level and more powerful schemes' (Athey 1990:37).

In my research I found that a greater awareness of the schematic concerns of the children observed, accompanied by a different way of looking at their activity – as form rather than content – led to an improved match between the needs of the children and the experiences offered in the classroom.

It appears that, as long as experiences offered are as far as possible non-prescriptive and open ended, children will take from them according to their need. It is important that adults, both parents and professionals, observe where children are and then respond spontaneously and sensitively to support and extend the child's learning. It is essential to maintain a range of experiences offering breadth and depth upon which children can draw. This does not naturally lead towards a skills based curriculum with a heavy emphasis upon predetermined learning outcomes. (Rice 1996:102)

Our early observations of Luke revealed that he was utterly fascinated by water and would spend part of each session enthusiastically filling containers and pouring the water out. He had no idea how to control this pouring and emptying and every day he was soaked, but luckily his mother was very understanding of his need. He seemed fascinated by the water coming along tubes, out of holes in bottles, through funnels etc. He would indicate his pleasure with energetic gestures, head nodding and accompanying noises. One of the classroom staff team would verbalise and comment upon events as seemed appropriate.

His mother told us very early on that he loved mechanical things. We observed this in school. He was drawn to anything that moved up and down, for example the lift on the garage or a Duplo crane. He explored paint, dabbing with painting equipment. He used hammers and enjoyed musical shakers. This interest in vertical – and horizontal – movement indicated a 'trajectory' schema (Nicholls 1986).

His other concern seemed to involve hiding objects. He was rather like a squirrel. We found orange segments secreted in his jumper, pieces of puzzle under a box on the floor and on one occasion, long after he had gone home, we found the class felt pens inside a doll's hat, inside the cooker in the home area. This was apparently an 'enveloping' schema.

At this stage, he was interacting very little with other children, although he did enjoy drawing the adults into his play. He was very happy when involved in self-initiated play and explored his interests in a variety of ways. We encouraged and supported these by feeding into the provision materials and experiences which might match his needs. We worked alongside him, responded as seemed appropriate and monitored his activity. He needed a high level of adult support to maintain his play and encourage appropriate responses. In 'free flow play' situations (Bruce 1991) he was able to practise, to struggle, to create and develop understanding. In the case of activities initiated by adults things proved more difficult. He was reluctant to cooperate, easily distracted and tended to disrupt the situation.

His love of water play continued, his attention to it unbridled. Over time he began to understand cause and effect, and to discover outcomes.

We organised different combinations of the equipment. We wanted him to try to solve problems; for example, by joining pipes together to enable him to direct the water and thus to notice where and how the water ran around the edge before running back into the tray. He showed an awareness of 'full' and 'empty'. He would indicate his findings by gesture and also noise, a shushing sound for water rushing along the tray, a movement of his hand from the bottom to the top of a bottle to show how it filled. At times he would watch other children and sometimes try to imitate their actions.

The pleasure he showed was unmistakable. Rosemary Roberts (1995) emphasises the importance of self-esteem in children's learning and the way in which in providing for schematic activity we are recognising and valuing the child and his interests, powerfully raising self-esteem.

> Instead of the likelihood of disapproval for playing in ways that seem normal and natural to them, we can make provision for children to play in the ways that they need to, safely and acceptably. In the warmth of approval self-concept grows. (Roberts 1995:100)

Luke gradually became happier in the class. His interactions with people and equipment were more appropriate. We regularly reviewed his progress with his parents in accordance with the Code of Practice. His mother made use of our Toy Library to support his interests. We agreed that progress was being made, although in terms of spoken language, this was minimal. He made noises and used some recognisable sounds – e.g. BIM, SSH, NEH (no) – but little else. We felt that his lack of speech made it difficult to assess some of his understanding and hindered his interaction with his peers. The level of attention and support he needed was not easy to provide in a class of 26 children with two adults. This is a recurring problem in nursery classes. When working with young children, the poor ratio of adults to children can make it difficult to support those with a particular need. Often, professionals focus upon the support which will be required once children move to infant school. In other words, the process of statementing focuses on needs in the formal setting of KS1 rather than on the needs of the pupil in the preschool. Extra support would be very welcome at these earlier stages.

By the end of Luke's second term, it was decided that he would not be ready to transfer to a reception class after the summer holiday and should, if possible, remain with us for at least an extra term. We would then complete the statementing process in order to ensure that his particular needs could be met for the next stage in his education. My approach to making provision is driven by the belief that children need opportunities to make sense of their world and the consequences of their actions in it. One of the most, if not *the* most, valuable things we can encourage in young children is the development of appropriate attitudes to learning. If children show persistence, concentration, an ability to tackle problems, make choices, respond to a challenge, these things will support learning throughout life.

> The ability to remember facts will be useful but the habit of trying out solutions, the knowledge that mistakes are a normal part of learning and the attitude that accepts and uses them positively will be crucial. (Roberts 1995:87)

If, together with the encouragement of a positive self-image and an awareness of the needs of others, Luke could be supported in developing these positive attitudes to learning, I felt we would be equipping him well for whatever he tried in the future.

To return to our observations, we noticed Luke was using his trajectory schema in mark-making, which was a new departure. He drew lines up and down the paper and then made marks which appeared to represent his name. He explored block play, building tall towers and then knocking them down. We began to work in parallel with other children and they would give a commentary for him. He enjoyed making sand cascade from flowerpots and using cars in paint to make horizontal tracks. His use of pipes and water became increasingly complex, with intricate connections of hoses and pipes which poured from one container to others at different levels. If one piece popped out he rushed to repair and to modify his design.

During the summer term he began to plan ahead, indicating his intentions with his own signs and gestures. He used occasional words, particularly 'yes' or 'no', but only when he felt there was no pressure on him. He became increasingly interested in writing, both his own marks and what he saw in print. He actively engaged with other children and was seen holding a child's arm trying to persuade them to join him in a game.

At the end of the summer term, a statement had been agreed. It identified needs concerning the development of expressive language, and suggested the use of support systems such as signing to support this development. The development of attention and listening skills, the development of fine motor and problem-solving abilities and work on social interaction were also targets. The objectives were to enable him to communicate successfully, to enable him to have success in learning and social opportunities and to support his development into an independent and confident young person. The statement included the provision for 15 hours extra support, and a nursery nurse was appointed to this position.

Whilst recognising the needs and objectives in his statement, there had been progress in all the areas identified, and we, as a classroom team, felt that it was important to build upon this. We continued to make regular observations of Luke and to use these to plan experiences which would support and extend his understanding. There is a considerable amount of evidence that this extension of learning is more likely to come from play which is central to the child's concerns, rather than those of the adult. Bruner (1985) uses the idea of scaffolding a child's activity, permitting him to do as much as he can by himself while what he cannot do is filled by a sensitive adult. Gradually, control is transferred to the child as they feel able.

In our work with Luke, the role of the adults, and in particular that of the support nursery nurse, was very much that of supporter and enabler. We tried to seize the moment. Wherever possible specific language work was done in the context of his own initiated play. This involved interpretation of his gestures with spoken language, appropriate encouragement of his attempts at speech sounds and increased use of Makaton signing. Early on in the introduction of signing, for example, Luke was 'driving' a pretend car. Liz, the support nursery nurse, introduced the signs for green and red – green for go, red for stop. When Luke was planning his intentions she would give him the signs needed to describe what he was going to do. In order to ensure maximum attention some work on signing was done out of the classroom and through adult-led activities, often using stories, games, songs and first-hand experiences for stimulus. Most work, however, involved other children in small groups, and Luke was encouraged to choose a friend to take part. In discussion with the speech therapist, it was felt that Luke needed work to develop his facial muscles. We therefore set up activities using the mouth to blow, and on one occasion did bubble blowing on the table. Luke enjoyed this, but so did many other children and the activity offered a number of learning possibilities – not least scientific, creative and aesthetic. In this way, we ensured that Luke did not feel isolated and was supported in his attempts at social interaction.

As time passed, we observed Luke working increasingly in collaboration with other children and spending increasing amounts of time developing an activity. He was skilled in block work/play, and showed a high level of involvement. He was more willing to cooperate in groups, but had some difficulty in taking turns – which we were able to work on. His signing skills increased. A major breakthrough occurred when he signed his plans and shared the song 'Ten in a Bed' with the rest of the class. He showed pleasure and satisfaction at displaying his skill, clapping his hands with glee. He began to use signs spontaneously in his play and other children signed back to him.

His mother was thrilled when he used signs at home. The support nursery nurse worked with her to extend her knowledge of signing. We worked to extend familiar vocabulary. It was more difficult to express abstract ideas and parts of speech other than nouns, but 'real' experiences like cooking or washing clothes provided opportunities.

A number of outings were planned for small groups of children including Luke. These included a visit to the city farm, a building site, the docks and a trip on the bus into town. These all offered rich language opportunities. Photographs were taken as a record of the event. Luke became very excited when he recognised the places he had visited, and the photographs were invaluable in enabling him and his friends to recall past events. His attempts at spoken language were erratic. He made noises and used occasional words: these were almost always spontaneous and if asked to repeat a word he became uncooperative. On more than one occasion when the speech therapist came to see Luke, she found him uncooperative and unresponsive.

Luke coped increasingly happily with larger groups. He showed greater enjoyment in stories and listened intently. He would choose to look at books by himself or with a friend. After a long time spent watching, he began to join in with movement sessions and to use large apparatus. Once he did, he was very enthusiastic and able to balance and climb and also to respond to stimulus.

His dominant schema remained that of trajectory and he was drawn to experiences which supported this. He enjoyed, for example, the story of the 'Spooky Old Tree' in which there is lots of action, particularly connected with up and down movements. He combined his interest in trajectories with his enclosing enveloping schema and also showed interest in rotation and 'going through'. In exploring work with water, he enjoyed the water going through pipes and funnels, he loved to get inside boxes or tunnels, he was thrilled with the ladder on the fire engine and loved to find handles to turn. Athey (1990) believes that over time, experiences are assimilated and coordinated through schemas. This coordination is seen as crucial for building up systems of thought.

He showed an awareness of what was going on around him and made observations about changes. On one occasion he helped to make pancakes and was aware of the fat melting as it got hot, and the way the pancake mixture changed consistency as it cooked. We had a leak in the classroom roof which gave Luke endless pleasure. He watched the drips coming into the bucket and his interest in the workman who came to repair it was all-consuming.

He expressed himself through a range of activities. His imaginative play developed and he explored more creative activities. We enabled him, where possible, to choose materials and make decisions about how he wanted to use them. His statement made specific reference to the development of fine motor skills. We noted the occasion, not planned in the conventional IEP manner, on which Luke wanted to take part in an activity involving plaiting wool. He did so and demonstrated good manipulative skills and a level of coordination which enabled him to achieve success.

Luke remained in the nursery for two years. After full consultation between all professionals, it was decided that he would continue to need specialist help in developing expressive language, and a speech and language unit accepted him.

In reviewing his time in the nursery there can be no doubt that he made tremendous progress in all areas of his development. I would like briefly to focus here upon just two aspects of his development, those of language development and attitudes or dispositions to learning.

After Luke had been in the nursery for about four weeks, it was recorded that he was able to communicate through squeaks and grunts, but was not using speech sounds. He indicated his needs through noise and gesture. He avoided eye contact. There was some evidence that he understood something of what was said to him. He found group story times very difficult to relate to and was rarely seen to pick up a book. He was very easily distracted and could not sustain interest in a story. At the end of his time with us, his profile records a different story. He was found to communicate enthusiastically and took pleasure in conveying his ideas. This had been greatly helped by the use of Maketon signing. He would initiate exchanges with adults and children, try to give explanations, plan ahead and predict outcomes. The number of speech sounds and words he used spontaneously was expanding and he frequently used 'yes' and 'no'. Luke took a great interest in books and knew how to handle them. He showed pleasure in listening to stories and could retell parts of familiar ones, paying attention to detail. He was trying hard to join in with rhymes and songs.

His approach to learning had also changed. I began this chapter with a description of Luke's behaviour at the time he entered the nursery. He spent only short periods of time at any one activity. He became agitated if other children were near him and would interfere with their play. His involvement appeared superficial, his use of equipment inappropriate and he was very easily distracted. At the end of his time with us he was exploring and participating in a wide range of activities with interest and enthusiasm. Whilst he still needed some support to keep on task he was showing an increased level of involvement and perseverance. He was making informed choices and was usually busy. He was coping more happily with new situations and responding to challenge. He appeared happy to be with others and to cooperate with both the adults and children.

As a practitioner, I believe it is healthy to maintain a creative tension between theory and practice, reflecting upon and evaluating practice in the light of growing theoretical understanding. There appears to be some agreement that knowledge and understanding can be reached by a number of different routes and that outcomes are very difficult to determine in advance (Drummond 1993, Hurst 1994, Bruce *et al.* 1995). Early years educators should bear this in mind when seeking to achieve a match between a child's needs, interests and experience. A developing professional expertise is essential if we are to support and extend children's development appropriately. The provision must be planned to meet both individual and collective needs. The nursery nurses and myself endeavoured to do this for Luke and for the class group in which he was set. Evidence and information gathered over the time he was with us show clear and significant progress and appear to vindicate my approach. There is no doubt that the child who left us displayed a sense of personal well-being and satisfaction in his learning. He was confident enough to share his growing understanding with others. Children who feel positive about learning want to learn more. It is my sincere hope that this has continued to be true for Luke. The important message here may be that IEPs with their set targets and prescriptions are not the best way forward for the youngest pupils with special educational needs.

Chapter 7

Small is special: making the best use of scarce resources

Veronica Lee

Small schools often attract special children. When we first used the Code of Practice we were amazed at just how many 'special children' we had in our small establishment. On to Stage 3 of the Code, we put the few children in the school who occasionally had hearing impairment, seasonal rather than permanent, and often worse in winter. Alongside them on the same Stage, we put all those children on the attendance register who received extra help from the Special Educational Needs Support Centre (SENSC) and those getting help from the educational psychologist. Those who needed extra help with literacy and numeracy – those who required a 'boost' to get them going – were placed on Stage 2. In different circumstances, these pupils might not be judged to need this level of support. Our intake is such that the majority of children are quite able, but these pupils were/are not reaching the same standard, hence a Stage 2 placement.

Our general judgement that, as a school, we tend to attract and support 'special children' has been confirmed by our recent Performance and Assessment (PANDA) report. We have 72 pupils and our PANDA report informs us that we have 24.7 per cent of pupils with special educational needs, as compared to the national average of 18.5 per cent. Whether our 24.7 per cent are whole pupils or simply 'parts of pupils' we have yet to discover. In fact we gained somewhat of a reputation in the area as a school that receives and caters for pupils with special educational needs.

The Code of Practice has been useful to us but it was, and continues to be, a costly business to implement in the school. Once decisions had been made about the needs of pupils, it required the involvement of the SENCO in taking small groups. She gave them a concentrated programme of work endeavouring to offer some one-to-one provision. In addition, she had time to undertake all the paperwork involved, conduct parental interviews and liaise with outside agencies. We had to budget for supply cover for one day per week to meet this demand: a significant expense for a three-class school with a staff of 3.4 teachers.

Maybe as a result of the reputation for catering for pupils with special educational needs, referred to above, or for some other reason, the parents of a very special pupil approached us. Their daughter was at that time being educated in a special school. They liked the school but felt it did not offer her sufficient stimulation. There was and is, of course, a feeling that such children will often make better progress if they are included in a mainstream school. It was the 'specialness' of this pupil that made it worth making her a case to consider. She was diagnosed as autistic, a condition which is difficult to fully understand and which often worries teachers and the wider school community.

After careful consideration we agreed that, providing extra support was available, she could attend the school for three mornings per week. It proved to be less easy to do this than we first thought. It required her statement being altered. This meant dealing with a variety of agencies outside the school which fell into the SENCO's area of responsibility, but it was a 'difficult case' for the SENCO to deal with. As a consequence, as head teacher I helped deal with the procedures and negotiated with the parties involved.

When she came to us we put her in a class with her peers. She rapidly became an object of fascination for pupils and staff alike. Her language communication skills were poor, but she demonstrated understanding. She found school work frustrating and often threw the most amazing temper tantrums. One of her more interesting habits was to hide herself under the computer table. To ensure that she was properly hidden, she usually wrapped herself in the sheet/dust cover thrown over the machine at night. She needed to be cajoled and coaxed to 're-enter' the class. But there were things that delighted her. She loved television programmes and looked at books avidly, although she was unable to read.

The rest of the children became very curious. We had the very difficult job of explaining to them that Mary, although often behaving in strange ways, was to be treated just like any other member of the school. Mary's parents brought into school a video of Mary's special school Christmas concert in which Mary was the star of the show. The children watched avidly, and in the end began to talk about Mary. They understood that Mary was 'special' but that this did not mean treating her differently. Like all children, she needed friends and more than anything else a 'normal' school life. We were surprised at how quickly the children accommodated Mary, how they intuitively understood her needs, but did not patronise her. After this, a sort of 'protection racket' ensued. Her classmates guarded Mary. She was protected from the gaze of teachers and other adults. For instance, on one occasion Mary emptied the class marble jar all over the floor during a wet playtime. In order to protect her from the wrath of the teacher, these were picked up and put away by the whole class. It was one of many incidents that indicated how well the children responded to this child with very strange behaviour.

After two terms, the three mornings that she attended the school were increased to five. By now she had reached the end of Key Stage 1, but it was fast becoming evident that she needed to be taught in a more rigorous way. Her language and social skills had developed beyond all recognition. She was able to hold a conversation with her peer group as well as with adults. Here social skills were such, that her temper tantrums were less frequent, and she was beginning to interact with other children in the playground. She was very unsure of the older children and quite frightened of them, so preferred to remain in the top playground, playing with the younger children.

Eventually, it was decided that she should join the school on a full-time basis. After much discussion in the staffroom, it was decided to place her in a class of reception/Year 1 pupils, although she was eight at the time. We judged that this placement would best help meet her social and educational needs. For instance, she was able to receive the same reading lessons as the most inexperienced readers, without it appearing that she was receiving yet more special attention. She remained in this class up until she was eleven, but joined in with other classes as and when appropriate – PE, for example.

During this time, she slowly learnt to read, write, count, do simple addition and some simple subtraction. Her language skills developed even further and she began to listen and think – she loved listening to stories and was happy to recount these to her parents. However, there were still lapses when frustration got the better of her and an odd chair would fly through the air! We were lucky, as the parents were always on hand and extremely supportive, so these instances were few and far between. We always insisted that if, for example, equipment had been thrown on the floor, she picked it all up. We felt that she had to learn to become responsible for her actions. She had difficulties in accepting that sometimes you got things 'wrong' – she felt that it was a slight on her and that her whole world was about to fall apart! This was a tremendous obstacle and took several years to overcome. Even now, she resents being told something is wrong, although she reacts in a far less violent way. She has learnt self-control.

When she was ten, it was decided to ask whether she could remain with us as a Year 7 pupil, adding an extra year to her primary school experience, instead of transferring to the secondary sector. We felt that in a stable environment, we could slowly introduce her to the next class, thereby making additional and appropriate demands of her, whilst at the same time getting her used to older children. It was also obvious that puberty was about to set in and, again, we felt that she would be able to cope better with this whilst in familiar surroundings. By then, our educational psychologist had changed, and the replacement EP was not keen on her transferring to a mainstream secondary school, believing that Mary would be better catered for were she to be transferred back to a special school. In which case, she would have had to leave us at 11 and not 12, as had been planned. Both the parents and the school were adamant that this should not happen. We had all put in a lot of time, commitment and effort and we felt that with an extra year in our school, she could probably remain in the mainstream for the rest of her education, provided the secondary school identified was not too big and had a good pastoral care structure.

An argument between the educational psychologist and the school ensued. In general, the LEA was ambivalent but happy to receive comment and argument from the school and parents. Both the parents and the school held their ground and eventually, with the agreement of the governors and the LEA, it was decided that Mary could indeed remain with us for the extra year, after which she would transfer to a small secondary school.

In September, Mary transferred to the next class – with Year 2 and 3 children. These were children she had worked with in the previous class, and she was academically at their level of development. She has found the work more challenging, but has learnt that even if she gets things wrong, it is better to try than to give up. She thrives on praise and understanding, and apart from her size (she is slight, but quite tall), no-one would think her different to the others in the group.

We also admitted another child, Susan, whose parents had moved from another part of the country and were keen that she attended a small school. She had been with us only a few weeks when we assessed that her behaviour and speech development were such that she would benefit from special provision. Whilst she was in the reception class, it became apparent that her language skills were such that she 'parroted' everyone. She simply repeated what was said to her. She was referred to the educational psychologist, who came to observe her in the classroom. Because of the school's reputation in successfully responding to the exceptional needs of at least one, the psychologist trusted our initial judgement and chose to observe her in the first instance, rather than undertake a battery of tests. After discussing Susan with the staff and the parents, he came to the conclusion that she too might be autistic. He referred her to the child psychiatrist who came in to observe Susan and to talk to the staff and the parents. The day he was due to come was a day of chaos. The head teacher's car had broken down, the AA were rushing round trying to mend it, the telephone was in its non-stop ringing mode, and in walked the school doctor. As the AA man came in to announce triumphantly that the car was mended and was rewarded with a hug, the doctor remarked, 'Och, I can see yurr a vairy tactile schule!'

He diagnosed Susan as mildly autistic – later it was suggested that she might have Asperger's Syndrome. Over the next few months procedures were set in motion to formally assess her in an attempt to get some classroom assistant support. Susan flounders if presented with any unfamiliar situation – she needs order and routine, otherwise, she finds it difficult to get through the day. For example, if she doesn't say 'good-bye' to her mother properly, she is upset for a good part of the morning. Her main difficulties relate to appropriate communication with others, and she is also given to making idiosyncratic judgements. For instance, she told me I would be unable to jump because I was 'too fat'. This was probably factual, but might not endear her to others! She takes things literally and has not developed the sort of social awareness that will enable her to interact easily with strangers and in unfamiliar situations.

Life in a small school is hard. The staff have to be everything to everyone. It is often difficult, but we are extremely lucky because we work well as a team. Everyone is willing to give up time to help the children in the school. Without this commitment, it would not be possible to meet the needs of the two children discussed above. Time is the most expensive commodity. Unlike in a large school, I have no protection from casual interruptions such as the AA man. It is the school's ethos, based on the belief that people matter more than procedures, that enables us to manage children with extreme difficulties.

The Code of Practice is useful, but if we were to treat it as tablets of stone we would be unable to make provision for pupils like Mary and Susan. We follow the Code of Practice and I think it is in the second drawer down of the filing cabinet…The Code of Practice does not guarantee resources. We have to fight for these and it is time-consuming – sometimes exhausting. But in the end we believe it is worth it.

How have we resourced the two pupils described above? Mainly through the school budget, of course. However, we now have some insurmountable difficulties. In order to reduce its over-stretched SEN budget, as of April 1997 our LEA has introduced a payment of £500 per year for each child with a statement of need. This is the equivalent of our year's educational consumables budget. What happens if we find we have a child needing formal assessment, as specified in the Code of Practice? Do we struggle on trying to teach the child with minimal support? Do we go for formal assessment and ask our PTA to fund paper, pencils and paints each year? What happens if we tell the parents that their child needs assessment and that the school is unable to afford it? Will the parents take us to court for failing in our duties with respect to the Code of Practice? Will we in future have to refuse to admit children who need to be assessed at Stage 4 because we are unable to afford it? The question has to be asked as to whose interests would then be served – certainly not the child's.

What happens when the green paper *Excellence for All* (DfEE 1997c) becomes a Bill and then an Act of Parliament? What happens if we have to take in children from the local special school (who would then need to be re-assessed as they would be transferring from special to mainstream schooling)? Accommodating six children reintegrated from special schools would effectively wipe out our school's premises budget.

My final thoughts are that whilst we want to include children with special needs as a matter of course, in order to do so we must have the resources. It is a matter of fairness that resources should not be taken from the other children in order to support pupils with special educational needs. Yes, I agree that the arguments for inclusion have to begin with hearts and minds, but the resource issue cannot be ignored.

Chapter 8

Managing to cope: special needs in a large primary school

Kathy Bale

Introduction

'Managing' (in the other sense of the word) is exactly how I sometimes feel at work. I am just managing to cope! It's a frustrating life, in that one never feels quite on top of things, always behind instead of ahead of the game – constantly trying to get to grips.

Updating the School Development Plan (SPD) is an annual event. There is often so much to 'develop' that it is difficult to prioritise and set achievable, realistic targets. We have internal influences guiding our development and this year we have put a lot of work into new systems for planning, assessment and record keeping. However, external forces cannot be ignored and the white paper, *Excellence in Schools* (DfEE 1997d), the Literacy Hour, the Numeracy Hour, forthcoming changes to the National Curriculum, the green paper on SEN (DfEE 1997c), the consultation paper and National Standards for SENCOs (TTA 1997) all need addressing. In January 1998, OFSTED descends on us, and as a result, all curriculum coordinators are trying to 'manage' as best they can, whilst preparing to be inspected.

Ours is an 11-class junior school, having three forms in Years 3, 4 and 5 and two in Year 6. This has been determined both by the infant school admissions policy and by the number of available classrooms. It is the policy of the governing body to keep class sizes small, and so we average 25 pupils in each. This arrangement has been at the expense of non-contact time for teachers, and next year we shall be obliged to squeeze three classes into two for financial and accommodation reasons.

The school building is old and rather cramped, and to provide a library, a mezzanine floor has been hung over two existing classrooms. The governors agreed to use part of the new library accommodation to create a base for learning support. We now have a very pleasant, light and airy working environment for groups with one-to-one teaching. This space is also used as the resource and administration base and there is a computer solely for SEN use. In addition to the classrooms and library, there is also a technology room.

The playground is small for 270 children and there is no playing field on site for games lessons. Enthusiastic parents have helped to make the playground area as attractive as possible by building a raised pond, outdoor chess set, play-station and benches. They have planted shrubs, window boxes, hanging baskets and planters, and the children have painted murals on the walls.

The children come from a variety of backgrounds. The majority are white, although there are 12 different mother tongue languages used by the children in the school. Some of these children receive input from the local authority language support service. The percentage of children with SEN this year is approximately 24 per cent. Eight children have a statement of special educational need and one child is at Stage 4 of the assessment procedure. Two of the children have full-time classroom assistants; one has a part-time classroom assistant and 0.1 teacher; one has a part-time teacher and the other three are supported by part-time classroom assistants. We also have one child, without a statement, who is supported by the peripatetic teacher for children with specific learning difficulties.

The school has a head teacher, a deputy (who teaches four days a week) and 11 class teachers. In addition, there is myself (part-time SENCO and support teacher for the children at Stages 1 to 3), eight SEN support staff, two office staff (part-time) and one welfare assistant.

I have worked in the area of SEN for about 15 years. After having my children, I came back into teaching through supply work and coincidentally began to get experience in special needs. I covered for a SENCO in a primary school, worked at the local MLD and EBD schools and eventually took a part-time SENCO role in a Church of England primary school. In 1994, I moved to my present school. In 1996, I completed a Masters degree in SEN, and I am presently studying for the RSA Diploma in Dyslexia.

SEN has a high status in our school and this is reflected by the fact that I am employed on one incentive point at 0.8 (0.6) for SEN (the LEA delegated staff resource is for 0.3). I am the SENCO and support teacher for children without statements at Stages 2 and 3 of the Code of Practice, and my role is described in the school's policy for SEN. Of my 0.6, 0.1 is designated for administration, although I have the flexibility to alter this as and when necessary. My timetable is also flexible and subject to change according to need. I work in a variety of ways: in class, with small groups out of class and with individuals in and out of class.

I have the luxury of not being a class teacher and being able to focus solely on SEN. This is not the case for all SENCOs in primary schools (Lewis 1995) and I feel that the more responsibilities one has to manage, the more difficult life has to become. The job style changes because responsibilities have to be delegated to other support teachers, thus increasing its management complexity.

The high status of the SENCO in school, the respect and support of colleagues, and her preparedness to work closely with others as a team, all go a long way to create a successful system of management. I have also found the broader support of the LEA and the help of colleagues in other schools to be invaluable. My own LEA provided the scaffolding to help its schools build their structures when the draft Code of Practice was first published in 1993. In this chapter, I shall describe this support, since it has made an impact on the way SEN is managed in my school and others in the borough, and demonstrates the LEA's attempt to aim for the kind of consistency that the Code set out to achieve.

Code of Practice – LEA

The borough has a very committed SEN inspector, and she and her SEN officers began working on the draft Code as soon as it was published. I attended a conference on the Code in London in June 1994, where there was a mixed delegation including inspectors, educational psychologists, head teachers, SENCOs and others. During seminars and workshops it became evident that my LEA was much further ahead than many in terms of how it had interpreted and operationalised provision for children with SEN since the 1981 Education Act. SEN is given a high profile and, therefore, much of what was presented in the draft Code of Practice was already being implemented in borough schools.

The LEA had used Warnock's staged approach to assessment and so it was relatively easy to adapt to the stages outlined in the Code. The LEA had always maintained an annual register of children with SEN from all its schools, a copy of which is provided for head teachers, the Special Education Advisory Team (SEAT) and school governors. Most schools, though not all, have had a special needs policy and a named governor in place for some time.

The Head of Special Services was quick to act upon the Code, setting up conferences and working parties to examine the new demands it placed on schools. Section 3:48 of the Code suggests setting up moderating groups to support the LEA, and in March 1994 our LEA had three groups covering:

- **Criteria:** for the identification of children with learning difficulties;
- **Proforma:** for IEPs, referrals etc.;
- **EBD:** guidelines for identification of children with emotional and behavioural difficulties.

These groups were not to be permanent, but were identified so as to help implement the Code of Practice. Group members included inspectors, educational psychologists, SEATs, head teachers, SENCOs and governors. A deputy head from one of the schools was seconded to help in the coordination of the working parties and in the dissemination of the resulting information.

I was a member of the Criteria Working Party for the primary phase: we decided to focus initially on Year 1 and Year 5. We were not starting from scratch, since Hampshire LEA is well known for its existing good practice and we were able to use its criteria as a model. These working parties produced guidelines for the identification of children with general learning difficulties, specific learning difficulties and emotional and behavioural difficulties.

For general learning difficulties, there are moderating sentences for Years 1, 3, 5, 7 and 9. These indicate the best a child can be expected to do at Stages 3 and 4 of the Code. An example of a moderating sentence would be:

Year 1: Stage Three: Writing:
attempts own writing but produces few recognisable letter shapes without adult help.

These sentences are intended to be used as guidance and not a 'pass' or 'fail' benchmark. Moreover, a child would not be expected to meet all the criteria for a particular stage of assessment before moving to another.

The guidelines for the assessment of specific learning difficulties offer a definition of dyslexia and list of likely characteristics followed by guidelines for statutory assessment. Guidelines for the assessment of EBD are given for primary and secondary phases at Stages 2, 3 and 4.

The main intention of the sentences was to achieve clarity and consistency across the borough, in line with the Code of Practice, and to give schools a supportive structure and reference point.

The proformas produced were for IEPs, referral to SEAT and Stage 2 and 4 referral forms. The proforma, personalised for individual requirements, is used by most schools in the borough. However, some schools, especially in the secondary sector, have begun to use SEN management software. This enables SENCOs to keep all SEN-related administration on a database programme which can be accessed by staff across departments. This offers proformas for IEPs, reviews, letters, referrals and SEN registers.

Training is a crucial issue, and in June 1994 the LEA organised a conference for SENCOs and provided supply cover. The day course was designed to give SENCOs an opportunity to create a 'model' policy which they could then take back to their own schools and personalise. This model was based on Circular 6/94 and drew on existing good examples of policies in place. Working together in this was a very useful experience and I am convinced that this made my task much easier back at school. Other useful outcomes of the conference included the outline for a 'Policy Action Plan', providing a time-scale for implementation and a borough policy on transfer from primary to secondary schools. The SENCO conference has since become an annual event and is supported by LEA SEN officers. Its present purpose is to provide borough-wide, cross-phase opportunities for INSET in which it is possible to meet with colleagues in order to share good practice, raise difficult issues and share transition information on children with SEN.

Subject panel meetings are held each term. There are separate meetings for primary and secondary phases, crossing every curriculum area. Additionally, there are meetings covering SEN and able pupils. These meetings, attended by the inspector for SEN, provide opportunities to organise INSET. As a result, talks on dyspraxia, differentiation, speech and language, EBD, the SEN tribunal and parent partnership have recently been organised.

The conference and the subject panel meetings provide a supportive network for SENCOs. It creates a sense of team work and prevents SENCOs feeling isolated in their own schools. In a small authority, it is possible for representatives from all schools to meet together. In addition, cluster groups also meet.

School – my role and the Code

Following the introduction of the Code, one of the first duties of the school was to re-design its policy for SEN. The work we did at the SENCO conference was extremely helpful because although we had a policy in place, there were new sections that needed to be added. The Code clearly gives the governing body and the head teacher responsibility for the policy (2:10), although the writing of the policy was delegated to me – with consultation processes built in.

The Code introduced new responsibilities for the school at Stages 4 and 5 in that the school has since become responsible for referral for statutory assessment. Previously, this had been done by the educational psychologist (EP) allocated to the school. Moreover, the school-based administrative work is now generated through the annual review of statements.

Beside the work involved in writing the policy, the main increase in demand on staff time has been the introduction of Individual Education Plans (IEPs) and their subsequent review. This is a very time-consuming process, generating many more meetings and resultant paperwork. Consequently, much of the remainder of this chapter is devoted to this aspect of my work.

The main challenge confronting SENCOs is that of improving the quality of education for children with SEN by involving them and their parents in proactive planning, which sets realistic targets for learning. The IEP will show how these targets will be monitored, reviewed and evaluated, and how and when targets will be re-set. The IEP will also show curriculum adaptations and modifications and it will describe methodology and organisation. It should guide the pedagogy of the teachers in responding to the needs of the children. An IEP should provide teachers with the information they require to carry out the individualisation of a pupil's work. It should also be a performance indicator. Through the IEP we can determine what input there has been. By monitoring the outcomes, we can alter future intervention for maximum efficiency. This is a great challenge, and one that we, in our school, are not confident that we have yet met.

To find a workable system for IEPs, it was necessary to provide a programme for staff training and consultation, which as SENCO, I organised and delivered. The first session began with some reminders about what IEPs should do and what they should include. The staff were then given a questionnaire designed to highlight concerns about the way IEPs were currently working. The next session was used to discuss the implications arising from the responses to the questionnaire. From this, we were able to formulate a ground plan. Children and parents were also involved in these discussions and their input was taken into account in devising the plan.

It was clear that the INSET had been useful. Previously, we had been writing IEPs for all the children for whom it was necessary. However, there were some concerns; for instance, some teachers were not managing their commitment, and such work as was being done was often not being recorded. There was also insufficient communication between individual teachers, so that sometimes, as SENCO, I worked with a child without the class teacher really knowing what we had been doing. As a result, follow-up activities could not be planned. At other times, the work I did might have been the only input a particular child might have received from one week to the next. This was obviously unsatisfactory.

Scrutinising the IEPs and the amount of support individual children were receiving brought to our attention the fact that most of the children were getting very little more than the others in the class who were not the subject of an IEP. One reason for this was that in an effort to make the IEPs practical and realistic, we were setting objectives which could easily have been completed in a normal class lesson. An example might be: 'to correctly form letters f, g and k – the class lesson – one per week'.

We also felt that there was insufficient time for consultation between teachers because, as stated earlier, non-contact time does not exist in the school and this means finding time during play-times and lunch-times or after school (the latter would not be an option for classroom assistants). As a staff, we agreed that it was essential to formulate a plan which would be supportive and which would enhance our confidence in what we were doing for pupils with SEN. Some of the solutions seem very straight-forward, simple and common-sense. But often, it is not until a situation is analysed that a solution presents itself.

It was crucial to the effectiveness of IEPs that they were accessible to the children, the class teacher and the parents. It was therefore agreed that each child from Stage 2 would have a work folder which would be kept in the pupil's classroom. In the folder would be placed a copy of the current IEP, together with all materials required to meet its objectives. A record sheet – for the use of those supporting the child – would also be kept in the folder. This would identify the work done, the date, and what the child achieved.

As SENCO, I would now see children once a week and would be able to use the record sheet to monitor the input of the class teacher and others. I could then provide feedback to teachers as to whether or not we were fulfilling our responsibilities regarding the Code of Practice.

This has not been an instant or permanent solution and we have to constantly remind ourselves of key issues and update our practice through regular staff INSET. It is also important that SEN has a high profile in the SDP and that governors are kept informed of the key issues.

Experience suggests that whilst children with learning difficulties have always been supported in our classrooms, the formal nature of the IEPs may result in the process of recording and reviewing being seen as onerous by class teachers. It is therefore necessary to involve other people where possible in order to provide teachers with support and encouragement. Some staff find it difficult to implement IEPs and we have to think of different ways of making the system work. To do this, some teachers may use quiet reading times. The child can also work independently, or be supported by a peer-tutor. Classroom assistants can also be delegated to upkeep IEPs, and at other times, parent helpers can be involved.

Children should be, and like to be, involved in their own target setting and to know what is being discussed about them. They are often very sensitive and feel depressed about being in a 'bottom set', and they do not want their friends to think that they need extra help.

Parents' involvement in their child's progress can be encouraged by their contribution in supporting their child in working towards IEP targets. However, for a number of reasons, this is not easy for them. Amongst the things that parents have told us are:

- they find their children don't want to take notice of them;
- other out-of-school activities get in the way;
- dealing with siblings means that they can't get the time;
- children are tired when they get home from school;
- they lack the necessary expertise.

Targets for children to practise at home therefore need to be manageable and meaningful.

We are presently adhering to the guidance of the Code of Practice by holding termly meetings to review IEPs. Parents are invited to these meetings. However, this is hugely time-consuming and we have discussed several ways of managing it more efficiently. Currently, we have a rolling programme of review, with two or three being completed each week – either before or after school. The advantage of this is that IEPs can be updated gradually and the process does not eat into teaching time, nor does it cost in terms of supply cover. However, it does mean that we are engaged in review throughout the year. In contrast, a neighbouring school has opted to allocate two full days for review meetings and parents are given a specific time to attend. Money is set aside to buy in supply cover for those days.

Some schools incorporate one IEP meeting a year and this is held during the parents' evening. Personally, I have never found that this approach has provided enough time to discuss the IEP in detail. The green paper (1997c) suggested a review of the Code of Practice and as a result, it may well be that schools will be able to respond more flexibly in their approach to this process. I would hope that such a review would result in a reduction of the termly meetings, with one taking place twice yearly – especially for those pupils on Stage 2.

As a staff, we have decided to formalise Stage 1 of the Code. Children at this Stage do not have an IEP, but we wanted to devise a proforma that would direct and focus our intervention for such children from an early stage. This form is reviewed termly by the class teacher and I keep a copy. It would be at this point that concerns would be raised about a child's progress, and the possibility of moving him/her from Stage 1 would be discussed.

Since the system described above has been in place, we have been working on the school's planning, record keeping and assessment policy. Short-term (weekly) plans have a section on differentiation. This reinforces SEN as a whole-school issue which needs to be considered across the whole curriculum. Weekly planning meetings for year groups provide staff with the opportunity to plan for any necessary modifications. There is also a section in the plan to consider the implications for support staff. This enables teachers to identify specific tasks for assistants. A copy of the weekly plan is given to the support staff so that they know in advance what will be covered in any given week, and their precise support role within that. Where possible, support staff attend planning meetings and offer input on ways of working with those children they support. Copies of weekly plans are reviewed once a term to monitor differentiation.

We have separate support staff meetings twice a term to discuss any issue arising from timetabling and to look at ways of working more effectively together. These meetings are often difficult to organise, since all the part-time staff are rarely in school at the same time.

Conclusion

In this chapter, I have described how the management of SEN is organised in my school. Present systems have evolved over the period of time since the introduction of the Code of Practice and this process will continue as we regularly evaluate progress. The role of the SENCO in this is a crucial one, made 'manageable' by the cooperation of all staff, the support of colleagues in other schools and the constructive involvement of the LEA.

Chapter 9

Two pupils, two SENCOs: same story

Peter Russell and Sheila Russell

Sheila Russell

As the SENCO of a first school of 193 children, I take a class of mixed Year 2/Year 3 children, 30 per cent of whom have special educational needs (SEN). During the year I am writing about, I had an interesting mixture of pupils who had academic, social and emotional and behavioural difficulties. I have a classroom assistant for 15 hours who works with pupils who have a statement of need. In addition, there is a stalwart group of voluntary helpers. I work closely with outside agencies such as our educational psychologist (EP), learning support teachers and a behavioural support teacher, all of whom are most opportunely sited in the building next door to us – they are always very helpful and cooperative. The relationships that I have forged have made the school the sort of place that educational psychologists and other support professionals will turn to if and when they are looking to place a 'difficult' child.

In April 1997 I was approached by our educational psychologist and asked to consider taking into my class, in September 1998, a Year 4 boy who had been in a special school all his academic life. It was felt that he was ready to come into mainstream but for a variety of reasons was not yet able to cope in a class with his peers. Roderick has moderate learning difficulties, compounded by mild cerebral palsy. He wears splints on both legs. He has had cleft lip and palate repairs which are ongoing. He has, in the past, had difficulty because of his small stature and fragile health. He wears glasses for short-sightedness. I was pleased that the educational psychologist had confidence in the school and in me. The psychologist thought we were able to provide a proper educational environment for the boy. As it happens, I know his family. Four of his brothers had passed through our school and I had taught two of them. More important for the placement of Roderick, I have a very good relationship with their mother, a formidable woman. Regardless of his needs, I felt a certain confidence because of my knowledge of his background and the fact that other professionals trusted the school.

The school could not accept Roderick without the permission of the governors, so the next thing I had to do was to make a request to the governors. They gave the idea careful consideration and agreed in principle to Roderick starting at our school, but only if resources were given to provide a suitable level of support. We needed more information about how Roderick actually behaved in class. We had plenty of documentary evidence on Roderick but I felt that if we were to offer him a 'good' educational experience we needed to see how he related to both the children and to other adults in his current school. I felt that this would not merely be of help in planning Roderick's programme but would be valuable additional information for the governors.

In June 1997 I visited Roderick at his school with the educational psychologist attached to our school. I watched him working with his class for half a morning. He was extremely sociable and talkative, but in my view, he did not seem to be tackling curriculum-related tasks. I came away with the view that Roderick was capable of achieving but that in his current situation he was not expected to work rigorously and conscientiously on curriculum tasks. As a result of my visit, we made arrangements for him to visit my new class when I taught them in July for half a day. This half-day was set aside for the children and me to become familiar with each other. As a visitor, Roderick would be in the same position as the other children. The visit went well and Roderick made himself very much at home, making friends and winning many hearts.

After these visits it was agreed that the educational psychologist and I, as the school's representative, would compile reports and complete documentation to be sent to County Hall. This paper was very significant: effectively it put the case for including Roderick in a mainstream school and made resource demands on behalf of Roderick so that he could benefit from his new placement. The county has a complex system of banding through which resources are delivered to pupils who have statements of special educational needs. Which band Roderick was placed in was critical, since it related directly to the number of hours of classroom assistant and midday supervisory help he would get. At this point, it was decided that he would need a Midday Supervisory Assistant (MSA), as he was still unsteady on his feet and prone to tripping and falling. Additionally, he had not been used to attending a school with so many other pupils and there might have been a danger of him being pushed over. Once Roderick had joined us, we were to learn very quickly that Roderick needed no-one to 'mind' him during outside play or in PE.

The school broke up in July for its annual holiday, and at that time I still had not heard from County Hall about the level of support Roderick would receive. I, as SENCO and prospective class teacher, felt that we had done all we needed and that at the beginning of the new term all the documents would have been processed by the county. In retrospect, I suppose I should have made more demands in July, but as we had just been through our OFSTED inspection, it was the least of my worries at that time!

A few days before we started in September, I went into school to see if there was any news from County Hall – but there was nothing except a form asking me to contribute towards Roderick's new statement. This was 5 September and he was due to start at our school on the 8th! I rang County Hall to see what was happening and it turned out that his previous school had incorrectly filled in the proforma. The information it contained seemed to suggest that Roderick could manage quite well in mainstream without extra resources. Rather than placing him firmly in the band that would give him the maximum resource, he was placed in a band offering the minimum. I did not ask how they thought that having been in a special school for four years he could make the change to mainstream with complete independence, but made it clear that without full classroom support and an MSA we would not be able to take him. I felt we had to take this tough stance in order to ensure that Roderick's educational experience would be maximised.

After many telephone calls and much argument, the county agreed a package of 100 hours of additional support pending a new report. We could use these hours how we liked, and luckily I had two potential workers on standby. Both had worked in our school before, one as a SEN classroom assistant and the other voluntarily in my class. They were ready to come in at a moment's notice, which was fortunate, because that is all they got. By the time all of this had been agreed it was the first day of term. One was to do 15 hours in the classroom and the other five hours MSA. As indicated previously, it soon became obvious that Roderick needed no-one with him outside or in PE lessons. He careered around the school cheerfully tackling stairs, falling over several times a day but laughing and joking as he got up, or was pulled up by one of his friends – of which he had made many, even in such a short period of time.

Academically, however, he needed more help and support. So, once again, I was on the phone to County Hall when I told them I was switching the five hours MSA to classroom support. This gave Roderick 20 hours per week of individual support for his academic work. Now I had a team. In retrospect, it is evident that the fact that County Hall had not responded properly in the first instance had left me with power to change the resource provision.

As we began to know Roderick well, we discovered that he was very adept at bargaining how much work he thought he ought to do. It seemed that he had learned the habit of work avoidance during his previous school experience. He seemed to tire very easily after any sustained effort. We took a tough stance and made it clear to him that he wasn't going to get away with work avoidance and that we expected a great deal from him. He soon accepted that and began to work hard both in school and out. He comes from a large, caring family for whom he is the special, youngest child. They helped him a great deal with reading and writing although we did have to gently persuade them not to (s)mother him as we were trying to teach him independence skills.

At first, the other children were very protective of him and he would sit there and let them do things for him. They hung up his coat, put his reading folder in the box, changed him for PE, including taking his splints off and putting them on, and practically carried him over to the main building (we are in a mobile). He accepted this in a wonderfully graceful manner with a huge grin on his face as if he knew he was fooling all of us. We intervened and made him do things for himself. And he quickly got used to the idea of independence and embraced it enthusiastically. It wasn't long before he did almost everything for himself. He progressed rapidly in every area and it seemed the more we demanded of him, the more he enjoyed it, and the more successful he was.

As part of the provision for his special needs he was supposed to have regular physiotherapy. No physiotherapy had been provided up to the October half-term, neither had we been approached by any physiotherapist. Once again, I made every attempt to make contact with a physiotherapist – ironically, they are based in a clinic directly across the road from the school. Meanwhile, we resorted to our devices. Fortunately one of our SEN classroom assistants had done some basic training in physiotherapy so she worked with Roderick on a regular basis. The aim was to strengthen the muscles in his legs, ankles and feet.

He was part of the class and so he came swimming. At first he made very slow progress. He was enthusiastic, but as his legs couldn't propel him he stayed afloat and gave the appearance of swimming 'on the spot'. We had no specialist advice but hit on the idea of getting him to swim on his back. To his and our joy, he shot across the pool like a wound-up toy, with a grin from ear to ear. This progress was accompanied by deafening cheers from his fellow class members. He hasn't looked back since. At long last, in fact almost at the Christmas vacation, we had a brief visit from a physiotherapist. We were given brief demonstration on how to exercise his legs and left with a sheet of instructions – we haven't seen her since.

All was going better than we could have expected, but the 100 hours emergency resource provision ran out at the end of November. As the date approached, we still hadn't heard anything, so we kept quiet and carried on regardless. We made the assumption that the resource would continue and that at some point County Hall would confirm this. The school was involved in the maelstrom of Christmas celebrations, carols, concerts, cards and nativity plays. In the midst of this I received a garbled message from the school secretary. County Hall had rung; they now had all the information for Roderick's new statement and they were not terribly sure that he met the criteria for the band that gave him the maximum resource. It seemed that in just over three months since he had left his special school his needs had declined dramatically and no longer required the level of support we had provided. My reactions weren't exactly in keeping with the Christmas spirit! I was on the phone to County Hall to speak to our local assessment officer. I went to see the educational psychologists in their den. I felt this was an emergency and I used up the 20 minutes per week non-contact time I am given for my SENCO role. Roderick got all the 20 minutes at the expense of the other 38 children with special educational needs. In effect, the school subsidised my involvement with the struggle for resources for Roderick, the head teacher taught my class while I got on with the interminable telephoning.

Yet again, I made it clear to County Hall that without support Roderick could not be accommodated in our school. I made the point that his progress in the short period he had been with us was dramatic, and this was due in part to the very hard work put in by his two classroom assistants. I made the point that not only would losing them affect Roderick's placement but a valuable and relatively inexpensive resource would be lost. I did not look forward to having to explain to the two classroom assistants that regardless of their supreme efforts they were not deemed to be essential. Privately, I could not understand why County Hall was quibbling over resources. I reasoned that apart from the very good arguments for inclusion it had to be cheaper to pay for 20 hours per week classroom assistant time than to pay for a place in a special school. What I didn't keep private was what I thought would be the effect on Roderick of the suggested cut in resources.

As I mentioned earlier, his mother is a formidable woman. Once she discovered that the cuts would affect the delivery of education to Roderick she would fight the system. The educational psychologist was forcible in supporting the case for the continuation of the researching. So County Hall was left in little doubt as to our feelings. In the view of all those involved with Roderick, except the County Hall bureaucrats, he was in the best place and it was essential that that placement was properly resourced. Even so, we finished another term with no resolution to the situation; we were in the same quandary as we had been in the previous summer term and the beginning of this one.

8 January 1998 saw the beginning of a new term and, at last, County Hall sent us a letter informing us that Roderick had been given 15 hours classroom support – five hours less than he had been given during the autumn. They even managed to get his name wrong on the advisory letter! Yet again, I was back on the phone explaining that he needed 20 hours to give him complete academic cover. Whether the man at the other end of the phone was worn out by now or full of New Year's cheer I don't know, but he agreed at once and said that another letter would be sent confirming this. This arrived about two weeks later – and ten months after the first request for us to take Roderick!

Peter Russell

Sally is a child who has now left my middle school and moved on to a high school. But hers is also a story of how a SENCO has to labour to make the system work for children with special educational needs. This is not an account of a battle with the system to get recognition of her needs; she had already gone through the process of assessment and its accompanying documentation and had been given the protection of a statement. It is more about struggling to find helpful information and ultimately finance and make the system work for her.

Sally has a physical disability, which hinders her learning: she is partially sighted. A number of outside agencies were involved. They were caring and conscientious and obviously felt they had Sally's best interests at heart. They described her condition and set out in great detail what action should be taken. They came to meetings and I attended meetings they called. Unfortunately, these meetings often resulted in me feeling *I* had special educational needs. For a long time, I seemed to be on the verge of finding information that I could use to help her but I always seemed to finish in a fog of misunderstanding. The technical descriptions and the medical jargon drove me to the dictionary, in fact the discussions often had the effect of confirming my ignorance. I could survive that, but conflict – or at least dissonance – loomed.

The problem began when my observations of her needs and my comments on the targets listed in her IEP contradicted those of the high-powered outside agencies involved with her. We shared many things but my concern was with the very practical. How could the school deliver what had been agreed and what was desired? No matter how carefully her conditions were described, how precise the judgements were, and how clearly set her targets were, they did not generate the resources necessary. I/we had followed the Code of Practice. Although I am not convinced of the procedure, in order to benefit Sally, I became 'number one good tick box boy'. The use of the Code of Practice had ensured that through its stages and reviews Sally was considered, assessed and monitored, expert agency help provided and problems worked on. However, when through this process specific need was identified and appropriate intervention approaches found, there was no funding.

In working on behalf of Sally, I found out what the Code of Practice does not do for a SENCO. It does not advise one as to how to write the sorts of begging and pleading letters that I needed to. With the backing and written support of Sally's parents, I wrote to the hospital specialist seeking help and advice. In the letter I set out the school targets and the action plans agreed – in this case, we wanted more information. I asked the specialist for information to further our understanding of her disability and asked for some comments on how the disability affected her learning. What we wanted was a clearer understanding of what her potential was. I received no answer. I tried again: no answer. I asked the School Medical Officer and finally got a reply. The specialist said that we were doing the right thing, but I was left with the feeling that more could be done for a child who was struggling and underfunctioning.

Sally was about to transfer from KS2 to KS3 when I decided to make strident comments on her annual review. I'd use the technicalities of the Code and force 'them' to provide more resources to solve the problem. I looked forward to the reply to the review, and was told Sally was progressing well and managing in the school. Meanwhile as a sort of afterthought, the hospital specialist revealed that Sally was now registered with a national organisation and they advised that there was a piece of equipment that would address her specific problem. Elation, but it was expensive and no funding was forthcoming. I wrote begging letters to a variety of companies but no avail. At last, thanks to a former pupil and his Shell offshore colleagues, some money was donated from a group of individuals. A sort of success, but now Sally has left for the high school.

Conclusion

Some thoughts occur to us both about all this. Commendable as the idea is to reintegrate children from special schools into mainstream – and I fully agree that in Roderick's and Sally's cases this was appropriate – the struggle for resources is interminable. Useful as the Code of Practice is, it easily becomes a technical instrument, SENCOs follow rules and procedures. It embodies a technicist and rational model of teaching but it ignores what we want to call professional artistry. We were convinced of Sally and Roderick's case as much from 'teacherly instinct' as from technical descriptions of their attainment and needs. It was this instinct that made us invest so much time in the struggle – and it was worth it, but will every SENCO have to fight the same battle all over again? Our experience is mixed. In Roderick's case it was successful but what about our responsibility to the other children? Will we do it again? In fact, just the other day an educational psychologist said to one of us, 'Sheila, there's this child in…'

Chapter 10

Spanning the divide: the SENCO and transition

Tony Duckett

Peter had a statement of special educational needs. He was placed by the LEA in the learning difficulties category – that is, his basic literacy and numeracy skills were poor and cognitive tests placed him at the lower end of the average ability range. Before Peter transferred from primary school to his new secondary school, I met with his parents in my role as secondary school SENCO to discuss their concerns. The parents sought reassurance that Peter would be able to cope with the classwork, the homework and the day-to-day demands that would be placed on his organisational skills.

In the summer term, I attended his annual review. Primary school staff, the local authority SEN officer, educational psychologist and parents expressed particular concerns about Peter's written work and organisational skills. What would the secondary school do to help Peter overcome his learning difficulties and to cope with the demands that would be made upon him? Discussions with our pastoral staff focused on the student's ability to cope with life in a secondary school. It was anticipated that Peter would require additional support to settle into his new school.

The main area of concern for the pastoral staff was the student's organisational skills (understanding and following his timetable, bringing the correct books and equipment to each lesson, completing the homework diary). There was a need to make staff aware of Peter's learning difficulties, to plan within-class support (he was not disapplied from any National Curriculum subjects) and to arrange an individual spelling and reading programme, as specified in the statement of special needs. The focus of the parents, pastoral staff, subject teachers and SEN staff was centred on the student's ability to cope with life in a secondary school, and in particular, the student's work and organisational skills.

Peter was described by primary school staff as a student who failed to concentrate on his work. He lacked motivation and he was easily distracted by other students. He apparently had few friends and he did not relate well to adults. Sometimes he was extremely stubborn and he could be rude to staff. I carried out a semi-structured interview with Peter before he transferred to the secondary school. He had already made a one-day visit to the school. Peter was encouraged to express his thoughts about the issues that concerned him. The interview attempted to cover several areas:

- Feelings about the forthcoming transfer to secondary school: Peter was excited about the technology and the science rooms. He expressed concern about school detentions, the need to work hard and his fear of bullying.
- Friendships: Peter said that he did not have any real friends. He stated his admiration for the achievements of one other student.
- Thoughts about school subjects and how successful he was with them: Peter stated that he was successful in a number of areas, including reading. He said that he was a good worker and that he was well behaved. This was not supported by other evidence.
- General attitude towards school: I was told about a number of bullying incidents and how it was Peter who always got the blame for incidents of name calling and fighting.
- Feelings about special educational provision: He said that he did not really need much help with his work. This was not supported by other evidence
- Interests outside school: Peter was not a member of any clubs (either in school or outside school). He told me that he liked to ride his bike. He often associated with younger children.

Peter did not express a liking for school. He appeared to have the hope that the new secondary school would, in some positive way, be a good experience for him. One can speculate that he hoped to leave behind his negative experiences for something better.

My concern was that we might neglect the development of Peter's self-esteem. Gurney (1988:5) states that '...there is a substantial body of evidence to suggest that school achievement is positively associated with the level of self-concept'. He argues that '...self-esteem permeates the child's whole life and potentially influences every single learning situation and action which he undertakes' (Gurney 1998:51). Maslow (1943) describes the individual as having a range of personal, social and intellectual needs. He suggests that one set of needs has to be satisfied before the next set of needs in the hierarchy can be considered.

Progression is from the personal, through the social, to the intellectual. When he is physiologically satisfied and he feels safe within his environment, where there are opportunities to grow in confidence, to develop independence and to develop a positive self-esteem through achievement, then the student is more likely actively to participate in opportunities to satisfy intellectual needs. Students are individuals who have individual personalities, experiential backgrounds, attributes and developmental characteristics. These all contribute to the student having an individual and unique self-esteem (that is how we value or estimate what we can do).

It can be argued that self-esteem is somehow associated with the student's social development, confidence level, ability to cope with new tasks, manner of communication with others, willingness to take risks and current performance levels. Students who have a low self-esteem may be fearful, anxious for approval, self-conscious, oversensitive to criticism and socially isolated. They may set low goals for themselves or unrealistically high ones. The student may underachieve and become frustrated about their learning. The targets set in the Individual Education Plan, therefore, may not be achieved because the underlying low self-esteem has a negative effect on the learning process.

If success in school is linked as much to psychological factors as to academic factors, if the social and the academic spheres of a student's life are linked together to the degree that 'success' in one is a condition of success in the other, then the emphasis on what can be taught, what can be learnt and what can be assessed, is very worrying. Gurney (1988:128) views 'self-esteem' as a 'meaningful phenomenon' that is 'a neglected issue'.

The transition from primary to secondary school can be seen as a discontinuity of experience. Students are required to adapt to a new and varied range of demands. When secondary school staff visit primary schools, the Year 6 students often express worries about the size and layout of the secondary school, making friends, the variety of subjects, the large number of staff, the organisation of their books and equipment, the difficulty of the classwork, the amount of homework, their fear of bullying and anxiety about getting into trouble with teachers. Students have a more formal relationship with secondary school teachers. In the primary school students often have a strong personal relationship with one particular teacher, normally the class teacher. There are often greater opportunities in the primary school for the student to receive individual attention and for the student to participate more fully in the activities provided. In a large school an unhappy student may receive only superficial recognition from a large number of staff. The student may have few opportunities to discuss their worries. Their worries may go unnoticed.

SEN staff are working against an educational backcloth that accentuates measurable outcomes. The National Curriculum provided for the centralisation of the curriculum. The primacy of subjects adopted a symbolic importance, and assessment methods were adopted to provide measures of accountability. Although some emphasis has been given to the use of formative as well as summative methods of assessment, the publication of league tables showing the examination results of students has focused the attention of those, both outside and inside the school, on the summative or end-product achieved by the student.

The Code of Practice has wide-ranging implications for the way in which schools operate. One of the main themes of the Code is the understanding of special needs as a function of social context – the context of the home and the school. This recognises that schools create – as well as meet – special needs. To assess and understand the needs of the student it is necessary to consider the difficulties of the student in relation to the learning environment. However, the Code focuses on the observable and measurable needs of the student. This is reflected in the requirement for Individual Education Plans (IEPs). Statements of special educational needs also require SEN staff to implement such plans. As a result, there has been a re-emergence of programmes, developed and used mainly by SEN staff, designed to develop specific literacy and numeracy skills. Many of the INSET courses now offered to teachers focus on the development of specific skills through the use of Individual Education Plans. The emphasis is on particular, observable outcomes and not on the processes that operate at school and classroom level.

Within the OFSTED framework for school inspections, student achievement is measured in relation to national standards. The focus is on the progress of the student in relation to evidence of preceding attainment. SENCOs need to demonstrate that attainment targets have been set for students. Such evidence will allow progress to be judged over a period of time and in relation to other students. The IEP will be one of the main tools by which SEN staff can provide evidence to inspectors and to others. It is not surprising that SENCOs, faced with such a degree of accountability to OFSTED, SEN Tribunals, LEAs and parents, are likely to select learning targets that can be specified and assessed and for which the provision made for those targets can be easily demonstrated.

Such pressures encourage SENCOs to focus on the progress of students in relation to specific skill-based teaching programmes. This may result in

SENCOs devoting more time to deal with the paperwork associated with the five-stage model and less time in considering the effect of the learning environment on the student and the student's self-esteem. There is a danger that the student is seen simply as a learner – in terms of what they can be taught. The simple view is that if it cannot be measured then it cannot be taught. I was concerned that the IEPs used within my school and those forwarded from primary schools were focused only on the measurable. Even behavioural targets specified measurable outcomes.

The concern then, was that the full needs of the student would be ignored and that the performance levels would be adversely affected if the student's self-esteem was ignored. Experience of working with students who have learning difficulties had cultivated a belief that these students were more likely to have a negative self-image and that their low expectation of themselves was associated with a low level of achievement. They can fail to fulfil their potential because of their low self-esteem.

National Curriculum subjects are planned through programmes of study. It can be argued that self-esteem needs to be developed through a similar structured approach. Steps should be taken to ensure that school is a positive experience for each student. Could a case be made for the need to make a deliberate intervention, through the IEP, in relation to the development of the student's self-esteem? The information gathered from my initial interview with Peter suggested that his self-esteem was poor. I decided to collect further data.

In meeting the demands of the secondary school, students benefit from the support of friends. A sociogram can show the status of a particular student in the group's affections and it can also indicate the atmosphere or affective nature of the group. Peter and the students in his form group were asked five questions regarding their friendship with the other members of the group. For example, they were asked to identify who they would choose to be with on a school trip, and if being bullied, who they would turn to for help. Discussion was not allowed. Each student was allowed to choose a total of three students, from within their form group, for each question. Peter failed to be chosen by any other student in response to any question. All other students were selected by a number of their peers and some students demonstrated a strong friendship with one other student. Peter only responded to two questions, selecting the same student for each.

It was an interesting feature of Peter's group that the boys and girls appeared to be grouped into two distinct factions (boys and girls). There were only three choices made across the boundary line between the sexes.

Within the boys' grouping there were two strong friendship cliques. The sociogram also indicated that the girls were more likely to be friendly with a larger group of other girls than boys were with other boys. Students may choose their friends on a wide range of criteria. The sociometric data appeared to suggest that students who exhibited differences within the group failed to be selected by other students. These differences included learning difficulties, membership of a learning support group, a low reading age, low intelligence (IQ) scores or having English as a second language. The evidence clearly suggested that Peter was socially isolated within a group where boys and girls appeared to be socially divided and where boys tended to be less friendly towards each other than girls were.

I then carried out a structured interview with Peter. He was asked to respond 'yes' or 'no' to a number of questions. Peter stated that his work and reading were good, that the teacher was pleased with his work and that he did not need much help. This was not supported by the information provided by the primary school staff or the secondary subject staff. However, Peter revealed that he was aware that he was 'not so clever' as other children and he stated that he 'worried a lot'. Other children, he claimed, were unkind to him and he said that people became angry with him. He expressed the desire to be 'someone else'.

Next, I gave each of Peter's form group a set of 30 cards on each of which was written the name of one of the students within their form group (including their own name). They were asked to sort the cards into three groups: 'the cleverest students in your form group'; 'the average students in your form group', 'the not so clever students in your form group'. The students were asked to place their name in one of the groups. They were given ten minutes, alone, to complete this task. This exercise provided evidence that the students were clearly aware of their relative academic position within the group. The students were able to successfully identify other students who experienced some learning difficulties. There appeared to be a significant degree of agreement about the students who were seen to be the 'cleverest' and the 'not so clever'. These groupings were supported by staff assessments. Whatever the reasons were for selection, students did appear to form clearly identifiable groups. Peter placed himself in the 'average' group but the information gathered from staff showed clearly that this was not the case. Peter was aware of his difficulties but he was reluctant to acknowledge this fact. Subject teachers had described Peter as stubborn, refusing to work, inattentive, uncooperative and having a hit-and-miss approach. There was evidence from teaching and non-teaching staff that Peter had no real friends and that he tried to gain favour with other students by buying sweets for them.

Playground observation revealed that he often ignored others and wandered off alone. He made insulting remarks to other students and had flown into a temper when provoked. Some staff reported that Peter was nervous and easily scared. He would tell on other students to try to gain teachers' favour.

Clearly Peter had concerns about himself socially as well as academically. He denied (to me and to himself?), however, that he was experiencing any difficulties or that he needed support. This suggested to me that Peter had a poor self-esteem. He seemed to be unhappy and in need of some success both academically and socially.

The evidence suggested that Peter lacked confidence in his ability to cope with the demands of the secondary school. He was anxious about his school work and he lacked confidence in his social relationships. Peter was socially isolated. The data appeared to support Gurney's argument that self-concept is strongly linked to academic achievement and that one influences the other. Peter appeared to have social and emotional needs but the targets in the IEPs had focused solely on his academic skills. Reference to developing Peter's 'confidence' was made, but the special provision failed to specify how this might be achieved. It appeared to be left to chance.

National Curriculum subjects are planned out with detailed schemes of work. It can be argued that to enhance the student's self-esteem, a similar structured approach needs to be adopted. However, teachers are not usually trained counsellors. We cannot fulfil the role undertaken by Child Guidance. Teaching staff are likely to be reluctant to accept an additional specific counselling role. I felt it important, therefore, to develop Peter's self-esteem through everyday activities that could be reasonably asked of teaching and non-teaching staff.

First of all, I met with all the staff who had contact with Peter during the week. This included subject teachers, learning support teachers and non-teaching assistants. I highlighted the role of self-concept and self-esteem in children's learning and I discussed my concerns about Peter. We agreed that there was a need to focus on Peter's success within the classroom and his relationship with other students. In particular, we wanted to focus on:

- the nature of the tasks set for Peter;
- the need for him to experience success;
- the need for him to be praised;
- the need for him to have a supportive group of friends;
- the participation of the parents in this initiative.

Support staff, pastoral staff and subject teachers met at a second meeting to examine Peter's work and to share examples of the tasks set him. We agreed that Peter responded best to tasks that fulfilled the following criteria:

- text should have a reading age of approximately 8.0 years' or needed to be read to Peter;
- appropriate spellings should be placed on the board;
- the teacher/support assistant needed to check specifically that Peter knew what to do;
- the task should be broken down into small steps;
- Peter required his progress to be checked every five minutes (even if it was only to ask if everything was fine).

Peter tended to work at a slow speed. We agreed that Peter should leave every lesson with a feeling that he had been successful. In other words, staff would make a point of praising him at the end of the lesson whenever it was appropriate. There was a consensus that the above points represented good teaching practice for all students.

It was agreed that Peter should keep a book of staff comments ('Target Book'). He was encouraged to collect positive comments from his teachers and from support staff. The form tutor met with him each week to discuss these comments and any concerns that Peter had. The Head of Year arranged to meet with Peter and his parents each half term to review the Target Book and to discuss examples of Peter's good work. An attractive folder was kept by the Head of Year in which Peter placed copies of his good work. The focus of these meetings was on the positive aspects of Peter's work and behaviour.

On the basis that self-esteem is enhanced if the individual feels that he is a member of a wider social group, we used the form group's personal, social, health education (PSHE) lesson to encourage the group to work together in a supportive manner. The form tutor and I devised groupings of students who were likely to accept and support Peter. Influenced by circle-time techniques, which emphasise that all members of the group are equal and important, we set tasks that required the group to work together in an interactive and cooperative manner. The tasks focused on the exploration of personal and social issues. We hoped that such activities would develop supportive relationships, empathy and the self-esteem of students. The tasks encouraged the students to talk to each other and only one member of the group was required to record the group's response: that is, Peter could participate and make contributions but he did not have to write (his literacy skills were very weak). It was interesting that other staff commented on how well the form group worked together in collaborative group work.

The form group was also targeted through the morning form periods. The form notice-board was re-designed. Each member of the group was asked to bring in a picture of themselves and possibly their family. Information regarding special achievements, birthdays, etc. was highlighted. A space was created to focus on a particular student each week and a sixth-form student helped individual students to prepare a small display about themselves. Within the first few weeks of the initiative, Peter was featured. Also, the form group was invited to make positive comments about one member of the group each week. The form tutor discussed opportunities to participate in extra-curricular activities with Peter. Peter was taken by the tutor to a lunch-time puzzle club (not simply informed about it). Here he was encouraged to participate in group board games. He was also asked to help in the school library for two lunch-times each week. These activities further developed Peter's relationship with other students.

I met with the lunch-time playground supervisory staff to inform them of our concerns about Peter. They were asked to look out for Peter at lunch-time and to make a point of chatting to him. Positive information about Peter was given to these staff on a weekly basis (Peter's progress, examples of success, etc.). Soon they were feeding information back to the SENCO about Peter (he was happy, unhappy, concerned about...). This raised the issue of how we involved our supervisory staff in school activities and how we inducted them into school life. Several have now become involved in the school's paired reading scheme.

The transition between schools is often an unsettling period for parents. It may be that parents of a child with special needs are likely to suffer higher levels of stress than to other parents. They are likely to have particular concerns about the pressures of a large secondary school on a student who continues to experience difficulties. The parents may believe that their circumstances are different from those of other parents and therefore they may have feelings of isolation. It was felt important that Peter's parents were given clear and early information about his progress. We wanted them to know that we took their concerns seriously and that their views were included in the planning and decision-making process. In addition to the half-termly meetings with Peter's Head of Year, they were encouraged to write positive comments in Peter's Target Book. They and staff were encouraged to keep me informed of all positive and negative comments so that I could act as a conduit between them. Brief telephone calls to the parents kept us in regular contact. Previously we allowed comments to build up and to be reported at end-of-term meetings. Peter's parents expressed their appreciation that they were receiving positive information from the school on a regular basis rather than waiting for periodic reviews.

The parents attended a session at school (with Peter) to discuss the use of the homework diary, what to do if Peter was unable to complete homework and how to help Peter with his reading and spelling programme. This led to the development of sessions for the parents of students who experience learning difficulties. As well as discussing the individual teaching programmes, the parents were able to share their concerns with other parents. This reduced some of their feelings of isolation. Meeting with parents in this way encouraged us to consider more regular parental meetings involving support staff and subject specialists.

Peter is now a Year 9 student who has developed his niche within the school. He still experiences literacy and numeracy difficulties and at times he lacks motivation and fails to participate fully in classroom activities. However, he is reported by parents and by staff to be a happier student than when he was in Year 7. He is cooperative, he participates more in lessons and his work is of a higher standard. His basic skills have developed to a functional level. Peter has a small but close number of friends and there is no evidence now of social isolation. There is a positive relationship between the school and the parents. Peter still meets each week with the form tutor and half-termly with the Head of Year and his parents to discuss his 'Target Book'. Group work continues to be a major feature of the form group's PSHE lessons. School reports are generally positive and staff comments now focus on his subject skills rather than his behaviour and attitude.

It is difficult to quantify the effect of the measures outlined above on Peter's successful integration into the secondary school. However, I believe that the subjective feelings of teachers and support staff are important. It is felt that our interventions have developed Peter's self-esteem and the measures have encouraged us to consider changes in our practice.

The nature of large secondary schools is to deal with cohorts of students rather than with individuals. SEN staff can be swamped under the pressures that impinge upon their work. Thus, there is a danger that students are seen in terms of teaching programmes and paperwork. As a result, there is little time left for teachers, support staff or parents actively to consider the self-esteem of the student. I believe that I found evidence to support the suggestion that students with statements of special educational needs:

- have concerns about their ability to cope with the demands made of them by the secondary school;
- are likely to have negative self-esteem;
- are more likely to be socially isolated;
- have few real friends;
- are aware of having a low status within the class grouping;
- have social needs that have a negative affect on their learning.

If this is so, then there are implications for all teachers within the secondary school – and especially for those staff who are writing IEPs and who are under pressure to devise and implement measurable learning targets. If self-esteem, self-concept and academic progress influence each other then teachers may do well to consider this statement by Nash:

> There is a sense, therefore, in which it can be said that schools teach hierarchical levels of personal worth more successfully than anything else. (Nash 1973:16).

Chapter 11

Establishing an effective relationship between SENCOs and educational psychologists

Lesley Kaplan and Alison Scott-Baumann

Working Together

This chapter analyses some of the many ways in which SENCOs and educational psychologists (EPs) can work well together. Working together includes the use of problem-solving techniques such as Force Field Analysis and action planning. We also believe in the importance of sharing values and beliefs and in making such factors explicit. One way of achieving this is to develop collaborative techniques for working with children and with adults, and another way is to develop structures within schools which can facilitate partnership with the LEA. We illustrate our story with four case studies and wish to acknowledge the support of the SENCOs[1] whose work is represented here.

Case Study 1: Neil

Neil, aged six, stands at the classroom door, smiling and holding the hand of another pupil. He and a small group of friends are on their way to the school's conservation area for a lunch-time treat. On the way, Neil's friends say how he has behaved during the week: 'He has played with me at lunch-time'; 'I helped him in class'; 'He doesn't squeeze my hand hard now when we're lining up.' Neil says, 'I feel happy.' His teacher reports that the intensity and frequency of his temper outbursts are much reduced in the past few weeks: 'He's like a different child, much happier.'

Neil has been the focus of a Circle of Friends (Newton *et al.* 1996) and it is the work of this group of friends, supported by their teacher, which has helped to bring about the change in his behaviour. In this case, Neil's group is part of a local project, led by the school's educational psychologist (EP), a teacher from the emotional and behavioural difficulties (EBD) support team and a health visitor, which is aiming to develop strategies within schools and within parent groups to support children who are anxious, withdrawn or depressed. In Neil's school, the Special Educational Needs Coordinator (SENCO) was responsible for negotiating with staff to identify a teacher willing to participate in the project and a pupil, Neil, who would benefit. The EP was responsible for training the class teacher in the necessary support skills and for running the first session in which the children identified as 'friends' explored with Neil the many things they liked about him as well as the things he did that made them unhappy. They then thought of one thing they could each do to help Neil change the negative behaviours – play with him at break-times; help him with his writing if he got stuck; tell Miss if Neil couldn't do something in class; stop Neil if they saw him doing something which would get him into trouble. Within the first session the EP's role was to manage the group process while simultaneously modelling the role for the class teacher. Subsequent weekly sessions have been led by the class teacher, each session reviewing the success of strategies, with the group thinking of new ideas to help and offering a chance for Neil to choose a game or a treat for the group.

As an example of collaborative work between EP and school this model has many benefits. It is a way for the EP to work alongside a member of staff other than the SENCO and to offer training 'on the job'. It relieves the SENCO of a direct piece of work with one child and increases the repertoire of staff skills. For the children, the involvement of a 'stranger' gives their group status and adds impetus to their work. For EP and SENCO there is the pleasure of an intervention which is invariably positive and which can provide a model of working which can be incorporated into the school's SEN policy.

Is this fanciful imagining of an ideal state? No, it's a real-life example which has been used as one of a number offered during training sessions for SENCOs in a course devised and delivered by local educational authority (LEA) psychologists in conjunction with a local university. The course was devised by the psychologists as part of the LEA's response to the nationally recognised need for SENCO training. This training appears to be required to help SENCOs undertake a role that is almost impossible to define with a range of responsibilities which seem almost impossible for one person to carry out.

Virtually every recent research report has shown that SENCOs need support to :

- make sense of national and local developments in SEN and to relate them to their own school context and practice;
- increase their knowledge base and fields of expertise;
- increase their sphere of influence, individually within their own school, particularly with policy decision makers, and as a networking team across the LEA (Thomas and Tarr 1996, Lewis *et al.* 1996).

A complementary aim of this course was the enhancement of the relationship between EP and SENCO. This requires certain issues to be addressed. For instance:

- the perception of the EP's role by schools – some schools see the EP as the 'agent' of the LEA and as a 'gatekeeper' to resources, some LEAs have established a purchaser/provider model for their psychology services;
- EPs not always being given access (as with some SENCOs) to decision makers in schools;
- some schools/EPs/LEAs focusing on statutory (individual child) work rather than taking a whole-school focus.

The content of this university-validated course was based on the Teacher Training Agency's proposed *Consultation paper on National Standards for SENCOs* issued in July 1997, and includes SEN legislation, SEN policy development; identification and assessment, record keeping, working with parents, working with colleagues, styles of support and the use of information and communication technology. It has involved SENCOs in research, discussion, reading and sharing knowledge, skills and experiences, and has offered models of working for them to apply in their own schools.

At a more detailed level, the training course involves them in a sequence of practical tasks which support them in different ways of thinking and doing, e.g. sharing expertise by demonstrating to each other a teaching programme such as Toe by Toe, analysing and developing their school policy documents and developing practitioner research skills for investigating an area of SEN (such as identification and assessment) which needs improvement in their school. There is also coverage of applied theories, e.g. application of a therapy such as 'Solution Focused Brief Therapy' to the school setting (Scott-Baumann 1996). These SENCOs also develop instruments for use in INSET. The Force Field

Analysis discussed here fulfils two purposes: it enables SENCOs to look at live issues and it also gives them a technique for generating debate with colleagues. As used by course participants, this exercise highlighted some of the issues to be dealt with in the remainder of this chapter.

Force Field Analysis

The approach is known as Force Field Analysis. It is based on the work of Kurt Lewin, a social psychologist who placed great value on the interpretative potential of 'Field Theories', which come from physics. Lewin described a system of dynamic equilibrium which explains how social systems can 'get stuck' because the negative and positive forces acting on them balance each other exactly. Although deriving from physical science, when applied to social sciences these forces can be emotionally based (needs, drives, aspirations, fears), as well as practical (resources, legislation, buildings, training etc.). Because it acknowledges feelings as part of the 'problem', Force Field Analysis is particularly helpful in situations where attitude change is important (Lewin 1935).

A Force Field Analysis requires group members to identify any forces, positive or negative, which influence the 'problem'. It is a visual technique in which forces are labelled with arrows on a diagram, positive (driving) forces on one side, negative (restraining) on the other, with the length of the arrows indicating the strength of the force.

The stages of the Force Field Analysis process are:

1   define the desired change and ensure that the group shares an understanding of the 'problem';
2   brainstorm all the forces, driving and restraining. Don't consider solutions at this stage. Try to evaluate the strength of each force (as felt by the individuals affected by the change, not just by the problem-solving group);
3   draw arrows of length proportional to the strength of each force and label them (see Figure 11.1);
4   draw up an action plan which sets out to remove or reduce the restraining forces. This is important because simply attempting to increase driving forces without reducing the restraints tends to build up a counter-reaction which can increase the resistance rather than reduce it. However, if the action plan can also include strategies for increasing the driving forces, so much the better.

Groups who have used the process find it helpful because it is visual and clear, acknowledges the emotional aspects of the change process and offers a structure for devising a focused action plan.

Course members were asked to use this approach to address the goal of establishing an effective/productive relationship between SENCO and EP. Using a very large piece of paper, the group came up with the analysis in Figure 11.1.

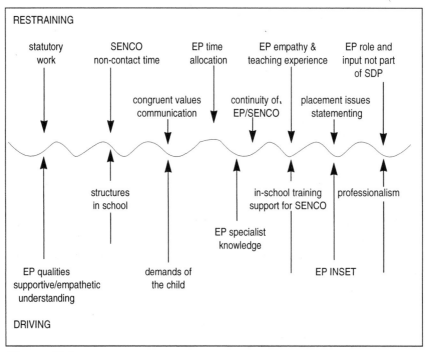

Figure 11.1

From this, they produced an action plan directed at reducing or removing the restraining forces. The action plan, as you can see, addressed some very practical constraints.

Action plan

Restraining forces

1 SENCO non-contact time

    (a) approach SMT to present a case for extra time; establish clear guidelines with them as to the SENCO role:

        • workload
        • time requirements

- their expectations
- more time would enable SENCOs to work alongside, or in consultancy capacity with, teachers to improve teachers' expertise in teaching children with SEN

(b) prioritise and timetable workload

(c) decide what can be delegated and do it

(d) set clear long-term targets

(e) establish an effective maintenance routine for monitoring/ reviewing

(f) make or build in time for emergencies

(g) share the workload, introduce shadowing by colleagues.

2   EP time/availability

(a) clarify EP's time allocation system

(b) plan for EP work at start of each term

(c) be clear about what is expected from EP involvement

(d) identify pupils who could be 'picked up' by other agencies

(e) negotiate project/preventative work from EPs.

3   EP role as part of SDP

(a) arrange joint meeting with EP, SMT and SENCO to identify areas where EP could contribute to School Development Plan

(b) ensure EP input is included as part of School Development Plan.

4   Statutory work

(a) review procedures at Stages 3 and 4

(b) agree date for completion

(c) implement changes where appropriate.

5   Continuity of EP/SENCO

(a) agree this is desirable but not always possible

(b) EP/SENCO to produce checklist for effective hand-over where necessary.

6   Communication

(a) carry out reviews of current communication systems

(b) set date for completion of review

(c) agree changes to effect improvement

(d) implement.

Thus, the analysis had helped the group identify negative pressures and arrive at strategies to address these practical obstacles. However, they had also identified effective features of the relationship between SENCO and EP, features which are less easy to action-plan for – but which are crucial to effective working. The group suggested the following actions to address the issue of congruent values:

- Ensure that time is spent discussing the wider picture of SEN in order to identify areas where values are shared/differ;
- Identify dates each term for these discussions to be continued.

This issue, the desirability of congruent values and the necessity of making explicit the beliefs and values upon which SENCO and EP working practices are based, is illustrated in the following case study concerning Alex.

Values and beliefs

Case Study 2: Alex

Alex entered her local nursery class (attached to the infant school) at three years of age, with a full statutory assessment and generous funding. She had virtually no intelligible speech and little apparent understanding of the situations in which she found herself. She was described as having autistic features in her behaviour.

The speech therapist worked hard in order to provide Alex, her parents and her teachers with support. At the first annual review there was much to be celebrated: Alex was by then talking coherently enough to be understood, she seemed more responsive to the context cues which enabled her to understand how to behave in the nursery and was making quite good use of Makaton in order to enhance her communications with staff and, to a lesser extent, with other pupils.

Towards the end of the review meeting, the EP became aware that Alex's Learning Support Assistant (LSA), June, was very worried about Alex's behaviour, despite the major improvements. In fact, June feared that the placement was about to break down. June had supported Alex's mother in teaching Alex how to behave in the local supermarket and was partly responsible for Alex's good progress. Further discussion and carefully targeted questions (asking about the timing and frequency of difficult behaviour) revealed that Alex and the LSA frequently locked into a battle of wills which resembled that of a two-year-old with its parents. This seemed consistent with Alex's generally delayed development, yet inappropriate within the context of a nursery class, in which many of the children were already learning how to learn. Further focused questions and elicitation of specific examples from June suggested that her supervision of Alex had became too structured in some senses: Alex's learning curve had been very steep over the last six months. Yet June, for her part, clearly feared that more freedom would allow Alex to regress to her earlier introverted, repetitive and autistic-type behaviour patterns. The available evidence did not support this. Three modifications of June's behaviour were therefore established in an attempt to change their relationship; less closely monitored time in the afternoon, more contact for Alex with other adult carers in the nursery and the planned involvement of other children in activities with Alex.

Two weeks later, staff reported that Alex was enjoying increased contact with other carers and continuing to make astonishing progress with speech and language. Her relationship with her LSA continues to be volatile but is less intense.

Embedded in this case study are several recurrent themes in the collaborative work between SENCOs and EPs. Firstly, important news or views may not emerge until the end of a meeting. Such views may come from a person with little perceived status and may be ignored for these two reasons. Secondly, it can take a relatively long time (in this case one hour of a three-hour school visit) to discover the hopes and fears which may be impeding someone from making an appropriate change in their behaviour. Thirdly, the EP found himself guiding the discussion although he would have preferred the SENCO to take the lead. The SENCO later said that she lacked the EP's skills and time, which made the EP feel perplexed as to how he could make a bigger difference...he felt he'd 'modelled' the problem solving well, applying clinical judgement to evidence which was available to both EP and SENCO at the meeting and that he had used different questioning formulae in order to solve the problem collaboratively.

On reflection, he realised that his perception of the situation was different from a reasonable outsider's interpretation of what was achieved. He had not made his thought processes accessible and was juggling with different hypotheses in his own thoughts while collecting more information. We can conclude that this was not perceived by the SENCO as an opportunity for active learning. Maybe this is partly due to the relative infrequency of EP visits, and the notion of the EP as 'visiting expert'. This conspires with the intensity of the workload in such a way that both EP and SENCO concentrate more on outcome than on process.

Yet, a case study such as that of Alex suggests to us that the EP may not always make best use of expertise (their own and that of others) in order to work creatively together. Perhaps we can learn by comparing the case study of Alex and the earlier case study of Neil and his Circle of Friends. The EP who was working with Neil used a modelling technique for training the class teacher. The EP who was supporting Alex did so too – but it was implicit and the SENCO did not adopt the modelled behaviour. Somehow, it is necessary to enable both EP and SENCO to be more open with each other. The EP could develop a working relationship in which the SENCO feels invited to develop an active understanding, not merely a passive appreciation, of problem-solving techniques, hypothesis-testing approaches and structured counselling methods.

Over-emphasis on the EP as the 'visiting expert', which serves only to create a dependency culture in some schools and resentment or cynicism in others, has been criticised for adding little to the notion of partnership. At the same time, the EP has a considerable amount to offer by being external to the specific context of each SENCO. For instance, the EP brings a perspective based on experience of working with SENCOs across a range of schools, some similar to, some different from, the SENCO's own. S/he is also part of the LEA's wider support framework and therefore has access to, and information about, the range of educational agencies which can be called on to support an individual school. Finally, EPs through their statutory work come into contact with a wide range of colleagues from other professional groups, especially health and social services, and can be helpful in bringing this perspective to bear in school-based consultations.

Earlier in the chapter, we talked about shared values. It is certainly necessary, but probably not sufficient, to have clarity about individual and institutional values in order to work effectively together. However, schools which offer robust structures to support such discussions have optimised their use of the valued skills of SENCO, EP and other external agencies. An example of such effective and planned use of these professional skills is described below.

Structures for partnership

Case study 3: multi-agency meetings

At a local comprehensive school, there are meetings every six weeks, attended by the Emotional and Behavioural Difficulties worker, (EBD), the Educational Welfare Officer (EWO), the SENCO, the EP, the school nurse and each year head. A 'problem' is brought to the meeting and an attempt is made to identify the best agency for resolving it.

Some possible solutions are discussed, a particular option is decided upon and a review date is set. The focus will vary – it may be an individual child, a group of pupils or even a whole year group. One outcome of such a meeting occurred recently when the EP and the SENCO worked with the whole staff to analyse and resolve concerns about the behaviour of a large number of pupils in Year 7.

The EP spent a morning observing the pupils and was able to confirm the staff opinion that some of the pupils were behaving badly and that morale among staff and pupils was low. A planning meeting was held with the staff at which people worked in small groups to identify the procedures they were already using that were going well. It then became possible to look at how to do more of these things that work, and for staff to consider the question 'What am I failing to do?' In a supportive setting, this planning meeting therefore had both a practical and a therapeutic theme. As a result, a consensus was reached about targeting the beginning of lessons with that year group. Three targets were chosen: being on time, taking coats off and lining up to come in. Pupils would receive a point for each target achieved, and for those who received a certain number of points, a letter would be sent home at the end of the week. There was peer pressure among the staff to be punctual and a dramatic improvement was brought about in the measurable motivation of many of the pupils.

This approach to multi-disciplinary work has been perceived as useful by many secondary schools, and is now being introduced to the primary phase in the local cluster of schools. It is hoped that it will make the best use of scarce resources and provide consistency across phases.

Case study 4: managing LEA provided SEN resources

While we are on the subject of resources…

An example is given here of work arising from SENCO and EP joint working at a management level in order to make the best use of LEA resources. The SENCO of an urban secondary school with a high level of Statemented pupils (9 per cent), the majority of them for pupils with EBD, and with (40 per cent) of pupils on the SEN register, was dissatisfied, not to say overwhelmed, by the task of managing the large amount of SEN funding which came into the school (and often left it) at unpredictable times of the school year. The situation is familiar to many SENCOs: a number of Learning Support Assistants (LSAs) were appointed on temporary contracts each of several hours per week. LSAs, and sometimes teachers, were appointed and dismissed as the SEN funding waxed and waned. The SENCO and EP, in conjunction with the LEA's SEN adviser, took an audit of existing pupils with statements, and numbers over the past three years, and proposed a radical overhaul of the school's SEN financial management structures. By regarding all SEN moneys as

i)   income provided to meet the needs of all pupils with statements and of as many others with SEN who could be included in support groups, and

ii) as relatively predictable, based on the pattern of the preceding years,

they arrived at a formula which allowed a degree of flexibility while maintaining core provision for the targeted pupils.

The resulting stability of support staff has allowed appropriate training for LSAs and support teachers to be implemented and the allocation of support staff to faculties and/or year groups, moving day-to-day responsibility for managing those staff to faculty and year heads, thus relieving some management pressure from the SENCO.

The model arrived at is as follows:

10% for appointment of 0.5 EBD teacher to allow consistency of EBD provision for statemented pupils across the school

2%   for LSA to support Talking Computer project

2%   one hour per day clerical support for SENCO (reflecting the significant administrative demands of this SENCO's post)

3%   administration and training for ICT innovations

2%   for purchase of ICT equipment

2.5% buffer for salaries

2.5% buffer for exceptional needs and for pupils leaving/joining the school

24% total top-sliced from school's total SEN budget (additional funding and statemented funding).

The remaining 76 per cent is used to provide :

• a key worker for each year group
• LSA hours for each faculty (faculties take responsibility for managing their own SEN LSA timetable).

The final task for the SENCO is to map the type of support each individual child receives within the SEN provision framework in order to ensure accountability in the use of statemented funds.

This model is now being used within the LEA as a prototype for other schools to adapt to their own particular needs and is an example of joint SENCO/EP work being incorporated as part of LEA policy development.

Conclusions

There seem to be at least two major tensions which cause us to focus more on outcome than on process and which therefore make it difficult for EP and SENCO to work together as they may wish. We need to consider them before seeking a way forward together. It may emerge that these tensions are not in fact the main cause of dissonant working habits, because causality is a notoriously elusive quality to prove. Nevertheless, we need to look at what we think is holding us back, because our beliefs themselves may function as self-fulfilling prophecies, predictive forces which allow us to generate obstacles in our own pathway.

So what are these tensions? One is the 'current narrow vision of education as curriculum delivery and of pupil performance as the achievement of curriculum goals' (Edwards 1998), and another is the role of EP and, with devolved budgets, increasingly the role of the SENCO also, as the definers of 'resource worthiness' (Dessent 1987). This often functions as a constraining force in the attempt to create a goodness of fit between the child's needs and the child's relative right to available provision.

It seems sad that both SENCO and EP may tend to feel that our effectiveness is determined more by our administrative output than by our child-centred input. This is particularly ironic in that, over the last 30 years, EPs have come to see themselves more as collaborative workers than as experts with mysterious measuring instruments. This change is related to the shift in late twentieth century psychology, away from the big, 'cold blooded' cognition theories (Butterworth and Light 1982) and towards a more 'warm blooded', sometimes Vygotskian, social constructivist approach which looks at thinking, learning and teaching in context more than it looks at a child-deficit model (Bruner 1986). Several generations of professionals have worked very hard to look at the child in context; examining aspects of the curriculum, the classroom and the school, which make a significant difference to a child's development and education. It is vital that EPs and SENCOs continue to understand each other – particularly over emotive issues such as ADHD. (Scott-Baumann et al. 1997).

However, recently there appear to be indications that a positive trend can continue. There appear to be real opportunities emerging from recent government initiatives for developing collaborative work between EP and SENCO, work which is based on reflective practice, skill sharing and mutual awareness, and understanding and respect for each other's knowledge base and expertise.

Many LEAs have already encouraged reviews of the way in which their psychological services operate, a process which rapidly gathered momentum after publication of the government's green paper *Excellence for All Children*' (DfEE 1997c). A thorough review of the purpose, functions and operations of LEA psychological services provides potential for the establishing of an easily recognisable, collaborative framework between SENCO and EP, founded on a more equitable partnership and clearly defined responsibilities. LEAs, such as those described by the Audit Commission as demonstrating 'high trust', foster 'shared values and a shared language' (Audit Commission 1998). Imaginative and dynamic LEA reviews can contribute to an ethos of shared values and language by unlocking existing expertise in both schools and psychological services, thus providing realistic professional development opportunities and reducing *ad hoc* approaches, without restricting individual initiatives.

LEA policies for SEN are increasingly seeking ways in which EPs (and therefore SENCOs) can be released from statutory work in order to allow a focus on support for pupils at Stages 2 or 3 of the Code of Practice or in research or project work on issues identified by the school. Service level agreements between the psychology service and the school are increasingly used in order to clarify expectations of and by the SENCO and the EP by establishing a 'contract' of rights and responsibilities on both sides which can be reviewed at the end of each academic year.

Partnership between SENCO and EP can, and should, be developed at many different levels of which we have given some examples. One is intervention with the individual child to improve the child's educational, emotional and social opportunities, and to support the teachers (Neil's story and Alex's story). Another level of intervention is exemplified by the in-service training of SENCOs by EPs, which has had a major impact on the working practices of both professional groups. Yet another is at the multi-agency level (case study 3) and the joint planning for management of a school's resources (case study 4).

All these, and the many other models of good practice, can help us to work together and to share our values and beliefs in order to support pupils and colleagues. This can be summarised in the words of Sue, a

SENCO: 'It is very much about facilitating a change in the environment, because in the end that is what is the most effective and the most far reaching for the pupils.'

Notes

1 Members of the SENCO course: Rosie Brydon, Sarah Cox, Alison Gunnell, Helen Heap, Robin Jones, Bruce Lang, Richard Lawton, Holly Lewis, Hugh Rees, Jane Sawyer, Jane Scott, Rachel Thomas, Jacintha Thurlow, Anita Trayner.

Chapter 12

The role of the SEN governor

Gillian Blunden

Introduction

This chapter considers the role of the governor with responsibility for SEN in the primary school. The major legislative responsibilities of the governing body in respect of special educational needs (SEN) are outlined, followed by an examination, in the form of a 'case study', of an SEN policy in a county infant school. This infant school serves a catchment area of considerable 'social disadvantage':

- less than 15 per cent of pupils on roll pay for school lunches;
- there are very high levels of unemployment locally;
- there are no owner occupier homes in the area;
- there are very few shops or offices;
- there is no bank and no dentist.

The school caters for children aged three to seven and 34 per cent of the children on roll are at various levels of the school's SEN policy, Stages 1 to 4. Stage 1 SAT results are below the national average. Its staffing is seven teachers, plus a head teacher, with six general assistants for 132 (plus 30 FE nursery) pupils on roll. It shares a campus with a junior school to which most of its children transfer at the age of seven. It seldom has the full number on its governing body.

The chapter continues with an analysis of the role of the governor responsible for SEN in the school, moving on to a discussion of the constraints operating against wholly effective functioning within that role. It concludes with a consideration of some implications of this position for improving practice.

The legislative framework: governors' responsibilities

Successive Acts of Parliament (1980 Education Act, 1986 Education No. 2 Act, 1988 Education Reform Act, 1993 Education Act and 1996

Education Act) have amended the composition of school governing bodies and increased their powers and authority. Governing bodies of county schools must now contain representatives of the parents of children attending the school, representatives of the teachers employed in the school, members appointed by the local education authority and co-optees drawn from the local business and other communities. The head teacher may, or may not, choose to become a governor. In other types of school (e.g. schools founded by religious bodies) at least some of the co-opted governors must be appointed by the religious body which founded the school. These are known as 'foundation governors'.

The main responsibilities of the school's governing body are now:

- to decide (with the head and LEA if appropriate) the aims and policies (including the policy for the education of children with special education needs) of the school, and how the educational standards of the pupils may be improved;
- to decide the conduct of the school and how it is run;
- to help draw up (with the head and staff) the School Development Plan;
- to manage the delegated budget;
- to ensure that the National Curriculum is taught, and to report on its assessment;
- to ensure that religious education is taught;
- to ensure that all examination results are reported;
- to select, suspend and dismiss the head and deputy head (who are employed by the local education authority);
- to appoint, promote, support, discipline, suspend and dismiss other staff (who are also employed by the local education authority) in consultation with the head;
- to act as a link between the local community and the school;
- to draw up an action plan after an inspection and to monitor how the plan is put into practice.

Clearly, the members of a school's governing body not only have a great deal of power and authority within a school, but are also required to undertake a lot of work as well. They are unpaid volunteers who receive no attendance or other allowance for their work as a school governor. They may receive travelling and other expenses in respect of attendance at governors' meetings and training events. The local education authority provides training for the various activities in which governors engage, funded from the governors' training budget which is now managed by each individual governing body. Whilst training is provided in this way, there is however no requirement for any individual governor to undergo any training whatsoever.

Governors and the school SEN policy

As indicated above, a particular part of the school's overall educational policy for which the governing body is responsible is the school's policy for the education of pupils with special educational needs. Since the report of the Warnock Committee in 1978, one of the main principles behind educational initiatives for the education of such children is that they should attend ordinary schools where appropriate. Governing bodies of ordinary schools, therefore, have important responsibilities towards children with special educational needs, whether or not those children have a statement of special educational needs.

The governing body should, with the head teacher, decide the school's general policy and approach to meeting the children's special education needs for those with statements and those without. This policy must be readily accessible, as must all school policies, to parents, staff and inspectors (Education [SEN] Information Regulations 1994). The governors must set up appropriate staffing and funding arrangements and oversee the school's work in this respect. They must admit a pupil whose statement of special educational needs names their school, although before naming a school in such a statement, the LEA must consult the governing body of that school. The governing body is accountable to the parents for their policy for pupils with SEN and must report annually to parents outlining how they have discharged that policy. An examination of a particular school's SEN policy provides useful illustrations of this work.

The case study school's SEN policy

SEN policy in the case study school was devised in 1994 and revised in 1997. It contains six aims.

Aims

- To identify and make appropriate provision for all pupils with special educational needs in the school context.
- To recognise there is a continuum of need and a continuum of provision.
- To provide access to a broad, balanced curriculum appropriately differentiated to meet pupil needs.
- To encourage close consultation and partnerships with parents.

- To initiate necessary involvement and support of outside agencies for individual pupils.
- To recognise the responsibilities and importance of the whole school staff in the daily operation of the special educational needs policy.

These aims are intended to be met through a whole-school approach (including the training of general assistants in SEN issues) to identification, assessment and appropriate provision through the five-stage model of support recommended by the LEA.

The model of appropriate staffing and funding arrangements to support SEN work in a school varies according to the governing body and therefore from school to school. Some bodies are able to fund a SENCO for release from general classroom duties for a whole day, others for half a day and some for no release at all. Much will depend on the governors' assessment of the volume of SEN work in the school and correspondingly its prioritisation of its LMS budget to meet those needs.

In the case study school, the SENCO is released from other duties for one half day a week in order to carry out her SENCO responsibilities.

The 'responsible governor'

All governing bodies must appoint a 'responsible person' from among their membership to ensure that all staff who are likely to teach pupils with SEN are aware of those needs. The 'responsible person' is often the head teacher – but need not be. If it is the head, then it is usually considered helpful for one other governor also to have a particular interest in the SEN work of the school. This 'responsible governor' is known as 'the named governor for SEN' in the school. In addition, the governing body may also appoint a committee to monitor the school's work for children with SEN.

Legally, the governing body is also required:

- to make every effort to see that the necessary special arrangements are made for each pupil with SEN;
- to make sure that the teachers in the school are aware of the importance of identifying pupils who have SEN and of providing appropriate teaching;
- to consult the LEA and the governing bodies of other schools when it seems necessary to coordinate special educational teaching in the area;
- to make arrangements to allow pupils with SEN to join in everyday activities of the school as far as is practical;

- to take account of the Code of Practice when carrying out these duties towards pupils with SEN.

In the case study school the duties of the governor responsible for SEN are as follows:

- to report annually to the governing body on issues relevant to the special educational needs policy;
- to monitor, on behalf of the governing body, the Special Education Needs policy;
- to be aware of the procedures for the identification of, and provision for, children with special educational needs within the school's SEN policy;
- to liaise regularly with the Special Needs Coordinator;
- to be aware of in-school staff liaison and outside agency liaison regarding children with special educational needs;
- to report to the governing body termly on the progression of the SEN policy and relevant issues regarding special educational needs.

As can be seen, the role of the governor who is 'responsible' for SEN is both interesting and varied. It is also fairly time-consuming. At a minimum, it requires the named governor to report on the SEN policy and the way it is being discharged in the school to the termly meeting of the governing body, and to answer questions. Typically, the report will contain: a review of the previous term's objectives for the SEN policy; a table containing the number of pupils at each of the stages, school-based and statutory; an account of staff development activities in respect of SEN; and the proposed objectives for the following term. The full governing body is asked to consider the report and agree the proposed objectives.

The named governor will also be responsible for working closely with the SENCO and other staff to develop further the SEN policy for presentation to the governing body. S/he is likely to be asked to be responsible for drafting that part of the annual governors' report to parents that refers to the ways in which governors have formulated the policy and carried it out. It is also likely that s/he will feel the need for further training in understanding her/his special responsibilities and will look to the school and LEA to provide that. Where the suspension of a child with SEN is proposed, the named governor may well find her/himself on the governors' panel to consider the suspension.

One of the major constraints operating on any governor responsible for SEN in the school is lack of time. All governors serve on a voluntary basis, and as amateurs, may or may not receive paid (or even unpaid) release from work to attend daytime meetings of the governing body. Even if the meetings are held in the evening, this can be problematic for some. It is especially true, however, that the SEN governor must be able to attend the school during opening hours for activities related to the school's SEN work over and above attendance at governors' meetings. Without a reasonably intimate knowledge of the school and a good relationship with the SENCO (which is explored further in another chapter in this book), the responsible governor is unlikely to be responsible enough. This is why, in so many cases, the SEN governor is likely to be the teacher governor (which then throws into question the objective assessment of the way in which the school is carrying out its SEN work), or a parent governor who is likely to be visiting the school at least twice a day. Adequate funding for such a role, including the payment of an attendance allowance, might rectify some of these difficulties. That, in turn, might remove money from the very children the system is designed to assist.

Conclusion

This chapter has examined, by means of an original case study of a county infants school and its governing body, the role of the governor responsible for SEN. It has highlighted the increased responsibilities that the governing body now has for SEN and identified the contribution governors may make to educational achievement by this means. It has also indicated aspects of constraints that operate on such a named governor. It is difficult, in the present financial and economic climate, to see ways in which practice might be improved, since the transfer of more educational funding to governing bodies is likely only to deprive the pupils of such resources. In many respects, reliance on governors' good will is the best that may currently be hoped for and achieved.

Chapter 13

Partnership in practice: governors and SENCOs working together

Stephen Grant

I have been engaged in local politics for many years. Unlike many school governors, I am accustomed to the nature of meetings and to the rules and procedures that govern their formality. In this sense, I have an advantage over the governors of many schools. While I think my political experience and my commitment to community involvement and the democratic process are important, I want to make clear the outstanding community commitment that governors make. The job is difficult and onerous. The process of creating and maintaining partnerships is not easy, but in my view very worthwhile. What follows, then, is a 'politician's' account of the partnership process.

How can governors and SENCOs form successful partnerships in primary schools? How long is a piece of string? More pertinently, how many primary schools are there in the local authority – in this case Bristol? For all 122, there is a method that works. What works in the leafy suburbs may not work in the inner city, and neither school may have a lot in common with one on a run-down outer council estate. It is to one of these last-named that I turn, not as an absolute beacon of excellence, but as an example of the way that governors and SENCOs can work together, the constraints on that relationship, and how one particular school and governing body have made the relationship work.

I begin with the one of the points made in an earlier chapter by Gillian Blunden. Governors are overworked and underpaid. The onerous list of duties and responsibilities placed on governors produces the first constraint likely to be placed on the relationship between governors and the SENCO. Most SENCOs are not governors. Indeed, it can be argued that the job of SENCO is so time-consuming, and in many disadvantaged schools so pivotal, that no SENCO would have the time also to fulfil the role of governor. Occasionally, the SENCO will be asked to attend a governing body meeting when special educational needs are being considered in depth, but usually, the job of presenting SEN to the governing body falls to the head teacher and the 'named SEN governor'.

The head's report, giving a factual update on the number and nature of SEN children, backed up by regular reports from the SENCO and the school's SEN policy, form a valuable source of information to governors trying to manage the education of SEN children in their school. However, they have a further invaluable resource, the named SEN governor. All governing bodies must have one. It is the link between the governing body and all the SEN work going on in the school. This could be seen as a 'spying' role, but if that is the case, then the governor has failed, the SENCO has failed, and staff–governor relations in the school are at a dangerously low ebb. It is far more often the case, in the majority of schools, that both staff and governors see the SENCO/SEN governor relationship as a partnership – an exchange of information and ideas that allows a key area of the work of the school to be highlighted within the governing body that has responsibility for it, while the SENCO can be kept directly aware of the thinking of the governing body on SEN.

The SEN governor needs to report to the full governing body regularly, but in a school with few SEN children, this may be only annually, when the SEN policy is reviewed. One cannot be prescriptive here. The governing body must be confident that its SEN policy is being properly implemented, and that the school is discharging its duties towards those children with SEN in its care. Governors would need to be able to communicate this confidence to OFSTED during inspection, while the inspection team would almost certainly want to speak to the SEN governor to ensure that s/he has his/her finger firmly on the pulse of SEN in the school. So, the SEN governor needs to have a good working knowledge of the SEN situation within the school, to be able to communicate this to other governors at the drop of a hat, and to have briefed them sufficiently often and in suitable depth to give them the confidence that the governors' brief on SEN is in good hands.

To achieve this, the SEN governor and SENCO need to have a good working relationship, based on mutual trust and respect, to meet regularly to establish and firm up that relationship, as well as to enable the SENCO to pass on information to governors. The SEN governor, therefore, needs to be in school regularly, especially if the SENCO has regular non-contact time. Ideally, the SEN governor should also be sufficiently distanced from both the SENCO and the children concerned to allow him/her to put critical questions, challenge the SENCO, and give clear unbiased reports back to the governing body.

Here lies the nub of the problem. The SEN governor needs to have a strong grasp of the issue, a familiarity with SEN in the school, and yet also needs to keep a distance from the staff and children involved that allows a critical assessment of the situation. Add to that the final part of the jigsaw, that most governors are overworked and are not able to give the level of commitment to the school that the SEN governor role demands, and a clear dilemma emerges for governing bodies.

As I have said earlier, there is no unique solution to this dilemma. However, my own experience at one primary school on a council estate with a high level of SEN can be put forward as one way of approaching the problem.

Initially, the SEN governor role was taken on by a co-opted governor in full-time employment. SEN Governor A had joined the governing body following exhortations in the 1986 Education (No. 2) Act encouraging members of the local business community to become involved in schools in their area. He himself admitted that his knowledge of SEN was not great, but he set about a rapid learning process and was able to offer a distanced view of the subject, increasing his critical assessment as his knowledge and experience increased. As a system, it was just beginning to bear fruit for the governing body when the individual concerned was transferred by his employer to another city and had to leave the governing body. Regular, clear reports were coming back to the governing body; governors felt their policies on SEN were being correctly implemented, and they had confidence that the considerable issue of SEN in the school was being properly addressed.

SEN Governor B was a general assistant at the school, also co-opted onto the governing body, to represent non-teaching staff, immediately bringing the SENCO/SEN governor relationship much closer. The new SEN governor had had and continued to have, in-service training on SEN to qualify her as a Learning Support Assistant, and allow her to be attached to certain named children through their statements. She had thus developed from a parent who had lived all her life on the estate and attended the school herself as a child, into a valuable member of the staff and governors, with a keen interest in SEN. Clearly, the governors now had excellent, accurate and thorough feedback on SEN in the school. Did we lose some critical objectivity?

I think not. Our new SEN governor, as a former parent herself, was fired with a belief that by and large SEN remained a mystical area to parents at the school, something they were afraid to ask about or explore further. Once the need for placing their child on Stage 1 of the Code of Practice was explained to parents, they understood and were supportive, but it was the initial breaking down of this barrier that was the problem between school and parent. As a former parent and long-time resident of the estate, SEN Governor B was able to bridge this gap, and felt an important part of her work was to relate to parents and relate parents' concerns to staff and governors, in a way which (she felt) parent governors with no SEN training were not able to do. This need, to identify with parents as well as work closely with the SENCO, gave her the ability to be a SEN governor that few other people would have.

I repeat, this is not a panacea. It works because members of the governing body make it work, appreciating themselves how the system functions and where SEN Governor B is coming from. It is made to work because in a small primary school with high levels of SEN, there are few options available for the SEN governor/SENCO relationship.

In conclusion, understanding is the key. Understanding on the part not just of the SEN governor and SENCO, but of the other governors. SEN is not an alien culture; everyone tries to make it part of their understanding of the school. In such a situation, a good working relationship between SEN governor and SENCO will work to the benefit of all, school and governors. SEN becomes too important to be left to just one individual; everyone must have a feel for it.

Chapter 14

Writing and implementing Individual Education Plans

Janet Tod and John Cornwall

Since the inception of the Code of Practice in 1994, schools have responded to the challenge to produce Individual Education Plans (IEPs) which 'identify needs, set specific learning targets, and assist teachers in planning suitable programmes in order to meet these targets and pupils' needs' (Code of Practice 1994, 2:119). The majority of SENCOs' inheritance from the Code was a responsibility for the writing and implementation of IEPs: 'in many schools a large proportion of SENCO's time is given to writing and reviewing IEPs...' (OFSTED 1997).

Whilst the increased workload experienced by SENCOs in developing and maintaining programmes for IEP provision should remain on the agenda for the proposed revision of the Code of Practice (DfEE 1997c), teachers have recognised some positive outcomes from IEP planning which include:

- the provision of a vehicle for the development of collaboration and involvement with parents, and a mechanism for enabling pupils to become more involved with their own learning plans;
- directing teacher attention towards the setting and re-setting of clear, educationally relevant targets;
- involving staff in the development and implementation of strategies to meet those targets, thereby improving and sharing classroom practice;
- harnessing available resources to meet those strategies;
- increasing the emphasis on the monitoring of pupil response to teaching;
- enabling a mechanism for providing clearer evidence as to the effectiveness of additional SEN provision (Tod, Castle and Blamires 1998).

OFSTED (1997) reports that 'in almost all primary schools, and in most secondary schools IEPs are prepared at Stages 2 and 3... SENCOs have worked hard to ensure not only that IEPs are produced but that they are regularly reviewed.' Given this acknowledgement of progress in relation to IEP development in schools, have SENCOs solved the problems inherent in writing and implementing IEPs? Is it time to redress the balance between administration, driven by accountability, and teaching? Have IEPs proven to be more of a hindrance than a help to pupils with SEN? Is the observation that 'The preparation and maintenance of IEPs is the area of greatest concern for the majority of schools' (OFSTED 1997) still applicable as schools prepare for their response to new government initiatives? Will the green paper's concerns for raising standards, 'shifting emphasis from procedures to practical support' (DfEE 1997c:5) and increased inclusion serve to reduce the requirements for IEPs? Or will the proposed reduction in statementing result in a return to paper-driven evidence-based IEPs for some SEN pupils? Will target setting (DfEE 1997a, 1997b) result in schools concentrating their resources on pupils at Levels 1 to 3 for literacy and numeracy and increase the number of pupils who are deemed to need 'extra and different' provision for literacy and numeracy via specific IEPs?

Whilst it is untimely to attempt to answer these questions, there is little doubt that the implementation of IEPs has done much to enhance the status of SENCOs and promote whole-school involvement in planning for teaching and learning for pupils with SEN. This progress has not been without cost to SENCOs.

This chapter starts with the premise that IEPs will continue to have an important role to play in securing monitored extra provision for some pupils with SEN. SENCOs are central to ensuring that the writing and implementation of IEPs is not a discrete activity which is nearing completion. It is an ongoing developmental process for schools that seek to meet the requirements for inclusive education for pupils with SEN. There is a consensus of opinion that further development of IEP procedures needs to be directed towards refining the paperwork, increasing the emphasis on how IEPs can best inform teacher planning and, most important of all, ensuring that IEPs have a measurable effect on pupil progress. It would seem to be helpful for SENCOs to ask 'to what extent are our school's IEPs *explicit, embedded* and *educational*?

Explicit IEPs...

'Schools need to give greater attention, not so much to the specific details of the IEP, but how it relates to teacher planning' (OFSTED 1997). During the initial development of IEPs, schools and LEAs interpreted the 'accountability' function of IEPs as being central to any of a school's IEP procedures. As a consequence, considerable time has been given to production of documentation, often in the form of detailed description of activities. In schools where IT is not used to support IEP writing, valuable time has been given to making handwritten adjustments to IEPs which involves the repetition of original writing. Whilst initially some inspectors gave credit to such endeavour, it is now recognised that there is a need for a change in the writing of IEPs:

> Schools are worried and confused over the way in which IEPs are used by inspectors and officers for the purpose of accountability. There is sometimes a feeling that they need to withstand legal scrutiny rather than a practical basis for individualised planning. (OFSTED 1997)

So how might SENCOs reduce the amount of writing needed for IEP planning? Some schools have invested in software to support IEP writing and maintenance (DfEE 1997c), whilst others have allocated additional clerical support to this task. One further way forward is for SENCOs to direct attention towards the fundamental purpose of the IEP. The IEP (plan) is a static written document which triggers action (process) from all involved in meeting IEP targets. It might be useful for schools to think of IEPs as being made up of:

- a brief document which is placed on record as the IEP
- a series of monitored actions informed from the IEP document. These are delivered and recorded by teachers, parents, pupils and specialists etc.
- a record card (pupil IEP) which may be owned and carried around by the pupil to record action which has been taken. This 'record' may be written in the pupil's workbook.

The IEP format should contain the smallest amount of information needed to trigger effective action. A simple IEP that conforms to the Code of Practice at Stage 2 could be:

Nature of child's learning difficulties: Emotional and Behavioural Difficulties.

People involved (by name): Class teacher, learning support assistant, mid-day supervisors, parent, pupil.

Strategies and programmes: Via agreed monitored action plans for all involved.

Targets:
- will be able to work co-operatively for a minimum 5 minutes per day on a structured task in the classroom setting;

- will demonstrate that *he is able* to increasingly seek attention from adults in a way which does not harm or disrupt others;
- will demonstrate that *he is able* to increasingly play a structured turn taking game with a peer or sibling whilst being supervised in an unstructured setting (playground and home).

Monitoring: Daily and weekly (to set sub-targets in relation to 'increasingly' [these may vary]).

Review date: At least termly. (Tod, Castle and Blamires 1998).

In this case, all concerned have agreed what they are going to do to achieve the targets. This, and the child's response, will be recorded in the class teacher's planner, in the Learning Support Assistant's monitoring diary, in the mid-day supervisor's log book, in a parental diary and in the pupil's exercise book or IEP record card. The amount of detail needed on the actual IEP document can be reduced simply because every person concerned with the IEP takes responsibility for delivering and monitoring their agreed support. For example, if in meeting one of the above targets, the parent or carer agrees to play a structured turn-taking game with the child and his/her sibling three times a week, then that detail does not need to be written on the IEP. The parent or carer takes responsibility for that part of the plan and reports only at regular intervals of review or when his/her programme of support needs adjustment. IEPs can also be reduced by evaluating them against Code of Practice Stages. Figure 14.1 describes how IEPs should not be compensatory devices which record detail of the curriculum differentiation and small steps programmes which characterise Stage 1 provision.

IEPs were designed to record the 'different and extra' needed by pupils in order that they make progress in their learning. Thus, if SENCOs examine their school's IEPs it is possible not only to describe the SEN population of that school but to compute which 'targets' occur frequently. This enables a re-think of what 'different and extra' means within the context of their school. The aim for the SENCO should be to reduce the number of IEPs by diminishing the need for 'different and extra' provision. The SENCO has a pivotal role in monitoring both individual and collective IEPs in terms of their purpose (see Table 14.1).

There have been conflicting incentives for IEPs. First, there is the perverse incentive to secure additional resources via IEPs. Secondly, OFSTED report (1997) that 'often the burden of maintaining IEPs is a major factor in the number of pupils placed on the SEN register at different stages', thus reducing the number of IEPs. In looking at their school's IEP targets, SENCOs could seek to reduce the 'writing burden' of IEPs by asking:

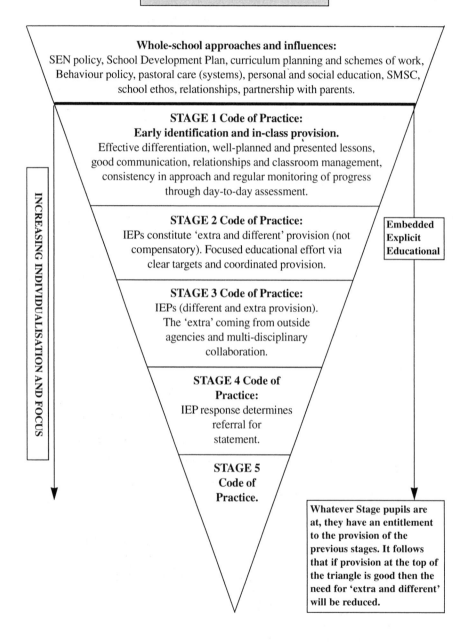

Figure 14.1

Table 14.1 The SENCO role in monitoring individual and 'grouped' IEPs

	The sum of all IEPs	IEP
Learner	Not applicable	Is my IEP helping me? Am I making progress (a) towards curriculum targets? (b) towards my own targets?
LSA or CA	Am I managing the IEP process for all my pupils? Am I making efficient use of resources and recording the progress made?	How effective is my delivery of the IEP? How well is the pupil responding towards IEP targets? Is this helping towards subject or other targets?
Class or subject teacher	Am I managing the IEP process for my pupils and the staff involved? Am I making efficient use of resources (human and otherwise) by evaluating overall/group progress?	How effective is the (or my) delivery of the IEP in all subjects? (a) towards IEP targets? (b) towards curriculum or subject targets?
SENCO	How effective is the IEP procedure for pupils in this school? Am I using *measures of pupil's individual and group progress* to evaluate this effectiveness? How manageable are the IEP procedures in this school? What are the implications for whole-school development?	Does the IEP procedure conform to CoP (and LEA) requirements, e.g. does the IEP need to be changed? Are the review dates being adhered to? Is everyone concerned clear about their roles and responsibilities? Has *sufficient focus been placed on progress and evaluative information collected to inform next stage of action?*
Outside agencies	How many IEPs is our agency concerned with in the school? Is our involvement with the school's IEPs effective and what are our resource implications? Can we evaluate the impact of outside intervention by measuring it against progress made?	Is our advice being effectively applied via delivery of the pupil's IEP? Is the pupil making progress as anticipated (a) in curriculum targets? (b) in IEP targets? *Are these mutually enhancing?*
Parents		Is my child making progress? (a) in curriculum targets? (b) in his/her own terms? Is he/she receiving the provision agreed on the IEP? Is my contribution valued and effective?
SMT	Do the school's procedures conform to the CoP (Code of Practice) and LEA requirements? Is the IEP procedure being effectively managed in the school? Are the pupil's making progress? How do we know they are (a) in the curriculum? (b) in their own personal development and IEP areas? Are the IEP procedures consistent with the school's SEN policy? Are the pupils receiving the provision described on their IEP? Can we measure resources used against progress made (efficiency) (a) for individual pupils? (b) for groups or year groups? What are the implications for (a) school development (b) budget and resource allocation?	Are individual pupils making progress as expected? Can we balance this against the individual resources required? Are there any problems with any individual resources required? Are there any problems with any individual IEPs which may be addressed by the SMT (e.g. parental concerns)? Are strategies cited on individual IEPs consistent with school policy (this arises in particular with EBD pupils)?

143

- Does the distribution and type of targets currently in place suggest that provision for individual pupils could be improved by development of teaching at whole school level and Stage 1?
- Do some pupils on Stage 2 share similar targets and need 'individualised' and not 'individual' provision which could be delivered via Group Learning Plans? (DfEE 1997c, Hardwick 1998).

Another strategy for the reduction in the amount of IEP writing is for the SENCO to implement an in-school training programme designed to promote the development of writing to support planning. Teachers need to be enabled to move from the existing assessment, recording and reporting framework which ends at 'reporting', into a framework that links with day-to-day planning. Maintenance writing needed for the implementation and monitoring of IEPs needs to be evaluative, not descriptive, and should always be informative. Briefly, what is required for further planning is *information* about pupil response to the IEP programme. What needs to be written down by those involved in delivering the IEP programme is the *outcome* of the self-dialogue: 'How did s/he respond to the strategy used?... 'What does that tell me?'... How might I use this information? ... What needs to be done now? There is also a need to monitor the impact of target achievement on overall classroom progress in a written style which informs any adjustments to planning (e.g. shorten sessions; involve peers; reduce pace; use visual clues; etc.). Tod, Castle and Blamires (1998) have developed 'ten key strategies' to inform this planning. These strategies could simply be photocopied on to monitoring sheets and dated to record progress and continuity in relation to the IEP. If IEPs are to be made more explicit, it may well prove cost-effective in the long term to give teachers the time and training needed to hone their writing skills in such a way that brief productive writing needed for IEP planning replaces retrospective reporting. Hopefully, this will free up more time to focus attention on the educational component of the IEP.

Educational IEPs...

The accountability and resource allocation function of IEPs has taken precedence over the educational function due to the need for schools to take note of how their SEN procedures would be inspected. As a consequence of the emphasis on procedures and accountability, IEPs have developed with a heavy emphasis on written detail and SMART (Lloyd and Berthelot 1992): Specific, Measurable, Achievable, Relevant and

Time-scaled. Support for the individual pupil has tended to be evidenced by compliant documentation and a restricted diet of targets, selected more for their measurability than for relevance. This weighted interpretation and response to the Code's guidance for IEPs is the reason for concerns about their effectiveness. The very fact that the IEP has a prescriptive set format is inconsistent with the notion that pupils with SEN require support which varies according to individual need. For example, the current IEP format has to record the nature of the child's difficulties: this has encouraged a return to labelling, with IEPs classified as 'behavioural' or 'learning' and with planning and target setting frequently based on pupil 'deficits'. Targets are always allocated to the pupil, even though for some pupils targets may need to be allocated to other individuals, in particular teachers and peers. The period review date carries with it the implicit assumption that this is appropriate for all those with an IEP, and does not allow for the responsive and adaptive changes needed for those pupils whose response may be very influenced by situational changes such as school or home factors, and for those pupils experiencing variable physical symptoms such as those associated with myalgic encephalo-myelitis (Stafford 1998). The emphasis on IEP procedural consistencies has thus tended to provide something of a straightjacket for those involved in meeting the diverse needs and inconsistencies in behaviours which characterise many SEN pupils.

One way of improving the educational effectiveness of the IEP is to direct teacher training towards the *principles* of target setting. Developments in IEP writing have included class and subject teachers being devolved the role of target setting. Further training could usefully be directed towards the role of targets in influencing pupil progress. IEP targets emerge from an assessment of the individual and as such have tended to fall foul of two pitfalls:

- they tend to be based on what the pupil cannot do;
- they are all too often compensatory and restricted to areas of literacy and numeracy.

They thus prescribe 'more of the same' but in small steps with additional attention provided by Learning Support Assistants. Whereas such targets can result in 'measurable' progress in the context in which they are met, it has yet to emerge whether IEP target achievement has a measurable effect on pupil progress *across the curriculum and in the classroom setting* (MacNamara and Moreton 1997). Thus, when design-ing and evaluating targets it is important to be aware that a successful IEP target should:

- have an impact on pupil learning in the wider curriculum context (see Figure 14.2);
- be intrinsically linked to long- and medium-term planning (OFSTED 1995a).

The ownership of targets is an important factor in the effectiveness of the IEP. Particularly, but not exclusively, in the case of behaviour IEPs, the adult in the classroom needs to clarify for themselves:

- Is this purely an individual problem?
- Is it a problem shared by a group of pupils?
- Is it a problem of whole-class management?

Parental and pupil involvement in target setting is also a powerful way of achieving 'relevance' and secures involvement in the process. Thus, a narrow IEP target such as 'will be able to write six c.v.c (consonant–vowel–consonant) words correctly' must be evaluated in respect of both achievement and impact on the pupil's written work in the classroom. A requirement that targets be assessed at two levels, achievement and impact, should address some of the educational concerns regarding IEPs (see Figure 14.2). Similarly, it might be useful for teachers to consider 'who owns the target'. Should the SMART target frequently seen on behavioural IEPs, 'must stay on-task for five minutes', be written on an IEP? Or should such a target suggest to the teacher that 'lesson planning must take account of the fact that five pupils in the class are as yet unable to stay on-task for five minutes'? This would prescribe an observation of under what conditions the identified pupils can stay on-task (e.g. use of visual strategies, peer involvement).

It could be useful to provide teachers with a taxonomy of 'targets'. These could fall into three categories:

- **Direct linkage:** learning outcomes = target.
- **Flexible linkage:** target = range of possible learning outcomes.
- **Indirect linkage:** target = an outcome which can be recognised but not prescribed.

Alternatively, targets may be classified as:

- access targets
- process targets
- response targets
- curriculum targets.

If IEPs are to become more 'educational' then the writing of the targets is an important and relevant starting point for development.

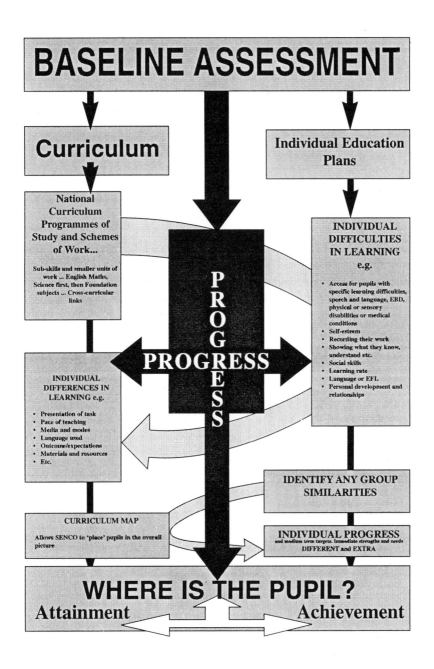

Figure 14.2

Table 14.2 Targets

	Increasing impact on attainment generally...		
	Target = Direct (learning outcome = target)	**Target = Flexible Linkage** (range of possible learning outcomes)	**Indirect Linkage** (outcome can be recognised but not prescribed)
ACCESS	Will look at teacher when she uses his/ her name	Will make it known to the teacher if he/ she does not understand	Will self-direct his attention to the task given to him
PROCESS	Will listen to and repeat instructions given personally to him	Will record information in a notebook when teacher is giving instructions	Will join in class discussion
RESPONSE	Will stay on-task for period of time set on his book	Will make a brief plan before starting to write and get this checked	Will respond appropriately to teacher instructions
CURRICULUM	Will mark 6 principal cities on a map of England	Will make maps and plans of a real place	Will enjoy geographical enquiry

Embedded IEPs...

What do we mean by embedded? This is a difficult area to define and quantify because it has to do with links, coordination, relationships (not just human but also strategies) and what is termed 'efficiency' by OFSTED (1995a). It has to do with the way in which resources, frameworks or systems are used and the way in which the various components of a system designed to track a pupil's progress are put into action.

When IEPs are embedded into the curriculum and into teaching and assessment, there appears to be better coordination of effort. When IEPs are not embedded, the vital connection between a pupil's individual programme, his progress and the planning involved, is lost. The result is likely to give the pupil a fragmented learning experience. This is why teachers sometimes say 'What is the point of this...? I know how well—

is doing! Do we really need all this paper?' Figure 14.2 illustrates the linkage and connections between whole-class based work and the individual approach suggested by IEPs.

Baselines are the foundation upon which progress can be mapped through IEPs. The Code of Practice points to collecting relevant and useful information. There is usually a great deal of information available about a pupil but it is often unfocused and dispersed. It is important that the collection and organising of this information involves a systematic process of sifting and prioritising. 'Baseline assessment' then become the SENCO's tool for defining a starting point for individual progress and progress within the general curriculum. Unless teachers know the pupil's starting point, there is no way of evaluating whether IEP targets are appropriately focused and whether their attainment has any impact on pupils' overall progress.

Figure 14.2 illustrates that pupil progress is of central importance. The 'Curriculum' pathway describes how pupil response can inform planning and differentiation. The response of the whole class enables the SENCO to place pupils with SEN on a curriculum map giving a view of their curriculum entitlement as well as their levels of attainment. The 'Individual Education Plans' pathway seeks to identify and address learning difficulties which require extra or different provision. In addition, an audit of these difficulties enables the SENCO to identify group similarities which must be addressed by adjustment or additions to whole-class provision (e.g. circle time [Curry and Bloomfield 1995]; class management etc.) The work on individual targets is designed to promote access to, and attainment within, the broad curriculum. At the same time, there are opportunities for attainment to enhance progress towards more individual targets. These could be taken, for example, by emphasising strengths (e.g. science, maths, or design and technology) in the pupil's work and using them to enhance feelings of capability and self-esteem when approaching an area of particular difficulty for that pupil, such as English. The links between an individual's progress, for example, in their study skills or inter-personal skills are important and will have an impact on progress in many areas of the curriculum. Behaviour and personal development (e.g. collaborative skills, affective development or other independent learning abilities) are often crucial to pupils' attainment or access, but only sometimes seen as cross-curricular.

The key point to note from Figure 14.3 is that the pathways are not discrete or linear, but interwoven and mutually dependent. Unless this linkage is nurtured, the expectations for inclusive provision, as prescribed in the green paper (DfEE 1997c), will not be realised.

Summary

Very often, demands emergent from central policy have created additional work and a conflict of expectations. IEPs have created conflicts for SENCOs in that important specialist aspects of their job have been marginalised whilst paperwork takes priority. *National Standards for SENCOs* (TTA 1997) reflects the complexity and importance of the SENCO's role and the inherent training implications. The green paper gives some expectations for coherence of policy in relation to meeting individual needs, but hopefully will move IEP development forward in an agreed direction. However, once again SEN provision has been *integrated* (*not included*) into the White Paper's 'standards raising' movement. Whilst mainstream pupils have been prescribed a Literacy Strategy (DfEE 1998a), SEN pupils are allocated limited mention in the planning documentation (National Literacy Project 1997) which states that IEPs should be the vehicle for provision. No doubt, another period of discovery learning for teachers and SENCOs will follow before attempts are made to address the conflicts for IEP development. These are inherent in the green paper's subscription to the rhetoric on inclusion *and* the white paper's prescription for targeted action for literacy and numeracy.

The IEP system had to be both rigorous and taken seriously at the outset if it was to be tested and tried as a mechanism for bringing increased efficiency and effectiveness to meeting individual needs. SENCOs have shouldered the burden generated by this period of change, but can take some comfort from the fact that the green paper (DfEE 1997c) now acknowledges difficulties with the implementation of the Code of Practice. Positive developments in relation to SEN have been triggered by IEPs; notably, collaborative planning and targeted and monitored provision. There now need to be adjustments to the thinking and writing of IEPs so that there is a balance between rigour and responsiveness. It is time to prioritise the essential educational function of the IEP. Inclusion can also be fostered by monitoring IEPs so that 'schools continue to explore new ways of developing responses that value diversity' (Ballard 1995). The logical consequence of any such development would seem to be a reduction in the total number of IEPs and an emphasis on practical monitored support. Clearly, SENCOs have the key role to play in developing these 'green' IEPs which aim to save paper and promote the development of educational ecosystems which foster the mutual development of teachers and learners.

Chapter 15

Compiling school policies for special educational needs: the role of the SENCO[1]

Jane Tarr and Gary Thomas

Under the 1993 Education Act, all schools must have a special needs policy, and this should have been completed and published by August 1995. Governors are also obliged to report to parents in their annual meeting on their progress in achieving the aims set in these policies. This chapter draws upon the results of research into the quality of SEN policies, commissioned by the DfEE and conducted by the Faculty of Education at the University of the West of England, Bristol. The research highlights several issues which are important for SENCOs to consider in relation to the formulation and review of a policy. These cover the following issues:

• consideration of who is involved in the review of policy and the audience for whom it is written;
• the involvement of senior management and class teachers in the review and evaluation of the policy;
• the process of collaboration and liaison with parents, external agencies and other schools;
• clarity of funding arrangements with clear budget statements;
• ways in which SENCOs can enhance their status in school and gain more time and support for the work that they do.

In brief, the findings show that policies are not necessarily presented in ways that are comprehensive or user-friendly. Most schools have relied on the short summary in the Code of Practice, which does not cover all the areas fully. The main findings of the enquiry are summarised below.

Aims and objectives

The central aim set for the research exercise was to assess the quality, user-friendliness and thoroughness of SEN policies published by schools and the degree to which they fulfil statutory requirements. To this end, the project examined the documentation produced by a sample of schools and looked specifically at:

- the proportion of schools that had published a policy at the time of the project (May 1996);
- how far policies reflected the Code of Practice, the Education (Special Educational Needs) (Information) Regulations 1994, and part 1 of Circular 6/94 (The Organisation of Special Educational Provision);
- how schools' policies compared with their LEAs' policies;
- the readability, accessibility and length of the policies;
- arrangements for development and distribution of policies.

Design sample

Nine LEAs; three shire counties, three metropolitan boroughs and three London boroughs (one inner and two outer) were selected to gain representation from a geographical spread of areas across the country, together with a sample of grant-maintained (GM) schools. Two hundred and fifty-two schools were selected at random, ten primary, ten secondary and five special schools from each LEA, together with three GM schools in each of these areas (or adjacent areas). Schools were asked for a copy of their policies and returns were received from 181 schools. This represents a return rate of almost 72 per cent. Follow-up interviews were conducted in 21 schools.

Procedure

All 252 schools were written to with a request for a copy of the school's policy. Included with the request was a short questionnaire asking about various aspects of the school: its status as LEA or GM, whether it was primary, secondary or special, its size, whether it was selective and/or denominational, and whether it was single-sex or coeducational. The questionnaire also asked whether the school had published a policy, when this was published and whether it was summarised in the school prospectus. A checklist of items was developed from the Education (Special Educational Needs) (Information) Regulations 1994, from part 1 of Circular 6/94 (The Organisation of Special Educational Provision) and from the Code of Practice. Because the criteria to be met appear in different forms in the various documents, they were grouped under 15 main headings, each of which had several subheadings. These 15 main headings are given in below.

1 *Principles and objectives held by the school:* whether these guiding principles and specific objectives are reflected throughout the policy
2 *SENCO's name and role* described in relation to others
3 *Strategic management and target setting:* the place of SEN in strategic management and how it will be implemented
4 *Admissions:* any priority arrangements
5 *Specialism:* special experience or skills, access for disabled pupils or a special unit attached to the school
6 *Resource allocation:* the principles guiding resource allocation, how this was used to discharge duties and how these were used to meet statements of SEN
7 *Identification, assessment and review procedures:* procedures for identifying SEN; procedures for assessment; monitoring arrangements; review procedures and staged procedures
8 *Curriculum:* strategies to include all children: access to National Curriculum described; curriculum development for SEN; strategies for differentiation; withdrawal/in-class arrangements
9 *Integration strategies:* how social integration was achieved; how curricular integration was achieved; how physical integration was achieved; liaisons with special school pupils
10 *Complaints:* how parents can complain and how complaints are dealt with
11 *INSET and staff development:* plans for teachers and assistants; with other schools
12 *External support:* sources of, and LEA agreements; other school staff involved
13 *External relations:* liaison arrangements explained, how the SENCO liaises
14 *Parents:* how working partnership is ensured: plans for partnership in place; how concerns are recorded; how parents are involved; how parents comments are included; how parents are informed and welcomed
15 *Transition:* between schools/to FE or adult life; SEN register; LEA proformas.

153

Each policy received was examined against the criteria in the checklist and for each of the criteria the policy statements were judged according to whether they merely mentioned (or did not mention) the criteria, whether they elaborated on the issue, or whether they explicated fully.

From the overall sample of schools, 18 policies were selected (two from each LEA) for detailed examination. The more detailed examination involved comparing the schools' policies with the LEAs' policies, assessing readability, accessibility, length of the policies (together with policies from the three GM schools), and conducting telephone interviews with SENCOs in these 21 schools to determine arrangements for development and distribution of policies. Following this, three schools were selected from the sample of 18. These were visited and semi-structured interviews were conducted with a group of staff in each. The aim of this exercise was to ascertain their awareness of their school's policy and how far they had been involved in its development. Ten parents (five whose children were at Code of Practice 'stages', and five whose children were 'unstaged') from each school were interviewed to find out about their awareness of and their knowledge about the policy.

Findings

There is great variability in the length and quality of policies and some issues are much better covered in policies than others. Areas that are superficially covered appear to be so because schools have relied almost entirely on the brief summary about policies in the Code of Practice. More detailed advice on the contents of policies (laid out in Circular 6/94) is not followed by most schools. For instance:

- three-quarters do not mention the strategic management of SEN provision
- two-thirds do not mention allocation of resources and only a very small minority of those who do mention it offer specific information
- external support is mentioned in three-quarters of the policies though the information is mainly in list form; the arrangements for liaison or the relationship was rarely described
- two-thirds do not give details on how parents should complain or how the complaint would be handled by the school.

However, some issues are well handled:

- nearly all policies describe a commitment to partnership with parents.
- 83 per cent of policies mention principles held by the school in providing for pupils with special educational needs

- 72 per cent give the SENCO's name
- 75 per cent specify identification, assessment and review procedures.

LEA support

Certain strategies promoted by LEAs (e.g. clustering) were more effective than others in helping schools to write policies. There was clear evidence that in developing policies, schools benefit from the shared experience derived from clustering with other schools. In one LEA which had encouraged such clustering, policies were of a consistently good quality. Encouraging clustering appears to be more effective than running courses or distributing information as a means of helping schools to develop policies. Where LEAs have provided examples of existing policies on which schools can model their own policies, it appears to have been particularly helpful to schools. Half of the SENCOs interviewed were not aware of the GEST funds which had been devolved to schools for the development of policies. Where there was knowledge about GEST fund use, SENCOs reported that it had been used to pay for courses or for release time for SENCOs to write the policy.

How policies are developed

Policies have generally been developed and written by SENCOs with groups of supporting staff. Governors have usually been involved only in ratification of the policy. LEA advisory staff have often been directly involved in meetings or in providing feedback on drafts. In primary schools, the process usually involved the SENCO preparing a draft with a few colleagues for discussion and amendment at a full staff meeting. In secondary schools there was usually a more complex process involving development of a draft by the SENCO and Learning Support Team (sometimes also involving Learning Support Assistants). This would then be commented upon by representatives from departments and/or the senior management team, usually as part of a working group.

Distribution of policies

Distribution tends to be to all staff and governors, though some schools limit distribution to senior staff or selected governors. While some schools had made policies attractive and readable, most policies were indifferently presented and tended to use difficult language and jargon which would make them inaccessible to most governors and assistants. On the Flesch Readability Scale, nearly all the policies were categorised as 'difficult' reading matter. Schools did not see the policy as a document for parents, but primarily for staff and governors. However, one or two routinely give a copy to prospective parents. None of the parents interviewed had looked at policies, whether their children had special educational needs or not. However, a small minority knew of the existence of a policy in their child's school.

The policies in practice

Most school staffs have found the process of writing a policy for SEN difficult but rewarding. Policies, and the process of writing them, are seen as useful in two main ways:

- protecting resources for children with special educational needs, by exact specification of special needs commitments and requirements. In the words of one head teacher, 'Publishing means you have to ensure that you can deliver.'
- as a working document in the development of good practice amongst new or inexperienced teaching or non-teaching staff.

Staff in most schools know about the policy (though not necessarily in detail), and find it useful as a way of making good practice for children with SEN explicit. Some schools saw policies as working documents, to be referred to by assistants and new staff. A few even gave detailed advice; for instance, guidelines might be given on classroom management. Others saw the document more as a statement about philosophy, commitment and existing practice.

Major issues

A number of major issues arise from these findings which it would be valuable for SENCOs to bear in mind, particularly when they are reviewing or developing their policies:

- the haphazardness with which policies meet the requirements laid down in regulations and the impenetrable language in which the policies are written – often seemingly, without consideration for an intended audience;

- the level of involvement of senior management in the implementation of the policy and in the review and evaluation of the policy in practice;
- the process of collaboration and liaison with parents, external agencies and other schools;
- the lack of specificity regarding financial information and the need for clear budget statements.

Finally, some suggestions are made about ways in which SENCOs can enhance their status in school and gain more time and support for the work that they are currently responsible for.

These are addressed in turn.

Reviewing the policy to meet legislative requirements and considering the intended audience

The statutory requirements are laid out in three documents, the Education (Special Educational Needs) (Information) Regulations 1994, the Code of Practice, and part 1 of Circular 6/94 (The Organisation of Special Educational Provision). The first document, the Education (Special Educational Needs) (Information) Regulations 1994, prescribes the issues which schools' SEN policies must address. They do not, however, prescribe the contents of the policies nor set a limit to the issues which may be addressed. Schools are free to develop their own policies in the light of their duties and functions and those of the LEA with regard to pupils with SEN under the legislation, in light of the Code of Practice, and taking into account the resources of the school and their most cost-effective use (Circular 6/94 section 23).

The checklist provided on p.153 could serve as a guide for SENCOs in addressing the key areas to be contained in a school policy as it brings together the variety of emphasis placed in all three documents alongside the actual legislative requirements. Schools have found this to be a useful framework. Each section should be mentioned, but the level of detail will vary according to the context of each particular school and the nature of the provision within the local community.

A policy should reflect the practice and aspirations of the whole school and in this respect it should be written by and accessible to all members of the school community. This will include teachers, governors, parents, support staff and external agencies working in the school. Circular 6/94 specifies that 'All teaching and non-teaching staff should be involved in the development of the policy.' In practice, involving everyone will be difficult, especially in a review. However, we suggest that it is often helpful to establish a policy development and review team, to include at least one governor (and preferably more).

Governors are important for two reasons. First, they are responsible for the policy and may be held accountable for its contents; they must therefore know what is in it and understand its implications. Second, governors – if they understand the implications of the policy and, more widely, the Code of Practice – may be powerful allies in bargaining for fair resources for SEN. On the question of audience, most policies examined for the purpose of this research project did not seem to have one specifically in mind. As a result, they were indifferently presented and used jargon and language that was difficult to understand. We would therefore suggest that in reviewing the policy it is important to consider who it is designed for, and that this should inform the presentation. The research evidence suggests that it is unlikely to be used by parents. Therefore, a short digest which refers to the full document can usefully be produced specifically for parents. The full policy should of course always be available for parents who request a copy.

Legislation does not specify audience. For the governing body, it must be seen as a document for which they can be held accountable, and therefore it is vital that they scrutinise it carefully and ask searching questions about its contents and review its success regularly. Indeed, they are bound by law to report annually to parents on the working of the policy. Development teams should have at the front of their minds the varied backgrounds of governors, and therefore try to avoid jargon and technical language. Beyond this, it is up to individual schools to decide who is likely to use the policy and to whom it will be distributed. In most cases, it is likely to be used by governors and staff and it may also be used as a reference document or a basis for staff development. It may celebrate particular strengths, successes or specialisms. If the purpose of the policy is clarified and decisions taken as to who will ultimately be reading it, it is likely that the final product will be produced in a way that is most accessible to that audience.

Management of SEN

The SENCO has the primary responsibility for the day-to-day management of provision for pupils with SEN, but without considerable involvement and support from senior management the work will be very demanding. In many cases, but not always, the SENCO is a member of the school's senior management team, and where this is the case, it has many advantages.

The status of the SENCO in terms of management reflects the importance placed on the provision for pupils with SEN. Such provision is best catered for where it is considered as a whole-school issue. In this respect, the role of the SENCO needs to be described in relation to other staff, management and the governing body. Ensuring that the school complies with the Code of Practice makes considerable demands on the time of the SENCO. Where this is undertaken as a whole-school issue rather than the responsibility of one person, there are many advantages for all concerned. There are aspects of the administration that could be taken on by class teachers, head teachers or non-teaching staff. The use made of information technology in the school could also be effectively directed towards the SENCO's work in areas of monitoring and assessment procedures. This can often save considerable time. This would need careful consideration by senior managers, particularly where such modifications require a redirection of funds.

The SEN policy should outline the role of the SENCO and list areas of responsibility. If management are involved in the allocation of responsibility and the monitoring process, then there may well be aspects of the work which can be shared amongst the staff. Class teachers are being encouraged to take on more aspects of the work in relation to pupils with special educational needs. The recently published *SENCO Guide* (DfEE 1997b) suggests that form tutors (in secondary schools) or class teachers (in primary schools) could be directly involved in the drafting of Individual Education Plans (IEPs) or the gathering of assessment information. The role of the SENCO may be more usefully viewed as that of coordination rather than of covering all the tasks associated with the delivery of educational provision for pupils with special educational needs.

Collaboration and liaison

Where LEAs encouraged schools to work in clusters to write policies, the quality of those policies was consistently good. Working collaboratively with neighbouring schools, therefore, appears to be a valuable way of helping to enhance practice. There is clearly a role here for the LEA in supporting such clusters to develop and in guiding their progress. Support from other SENCOs from neighbouring schools can enable individual schools to reflect upon their own practice and share experiences with others. There are three particular areas of liaison between schools that could immediately be beneficial. These are: accessing special school provision; liaison and involvement of parents in provision for pupils with SEN; and the process of working with external agencies.

Throughout the checklist for SEN policies (p.153) there are aspects which would benefit from collaboration and liaison with other schools. Circular 6/94 identifies several aspects that require liaison with other schools: the school's SEN policy should set out any arrangements whereby the school draws upon the staff and resources of other schools, including special schools, to help provide for pupils with special educational needs. Similarly, the policy should explain any arrangements which the school makes for integrating pupils from special schools (Section 53 Circular 6/94).

The integration of pupils with SEN could involve liaison with special schools in relation to the staged inclusion of pupils socially, physically and in various aspects of curricular provision. Staff development organised across schools in a geographical area can ensure that costs are shared and kept to the minimum. Support from other schools is highlighted as a further source for schools to draw upon in developing their provision for pupils with SEN, and the ways in which this liaison takes place need to be outlined. The transition of pupils between schools is an important aspect for pupils with SEN whether this is from primary to secondary, special to mainstream, school to FE college or into adult life. The quality of the liaison processes between schools regarding records and arrangements can be crucial for pupils with SEN.

Partnership with parents is a further aspect of collaboration that is required of all schools – but this may be even more pertinent for pupils with SEN. The work of the SENCO can be greatly reduced if procedures for this partnership are developed across the whole school, for all pupils. Subsequent refinement for monitoring progress and reviews for specific pupils can make use of the systems and frameworks which will already be in place within the school. This is invariably enhanced when senior management is actively involved in the process.

The process of liaison with a range of external agencies is an important and time-consuming element of the SENCO's role. Circular 6/94 outlines how schools should account for their sources of external support and the nature of their liaison with health, social services and educational welfare services as well as voluntary organisations:

> ...state the school's arrangements for securing access to external support for pupils with SENs...explain the sources from which the school seeks external specialist support and any service level agreement with the LEA. (Circular 6/94, Section 51)

It is often helpful when SENCOs set out arrangements for the process of liaison that are clear, realistic and useful to those involved. The nature of the relationship needs to be carefully outlined if the input from other professionals is to be maximised. The majority of schools' SEN policies examined for the purpose of this research tended to present a list of external agencies that were available to draw upon, often providing names of key personnel and telephone numbers. It was very rare to find a description of the relationship regarding level of contact and service level agreements. This is important if schools are to feel supported by external agencies and, indeed, if external agencies are to be able to deliver the support required by schools. One of the schools in the survey outlined the timetable for the educational psychologist's visits across the year, linking this into the work of reviews and staff development in specific areas. This level of detail is complex and may not be readily achievable but where it is in place, it can result in clearer understanding of roles and responsibilities and more efficient use of time.

SENCOs often access support through telephone conversations, which can reduce the need for time-consuming visits. This also needs to be carefully organised if maximum value is to be made of it. In some of the schools studies, the head teacher was responsible for external liaison. This took some of the responsibility from the SENCO. Careful planning and clear arrangements for external liaison are important and may require the involvement of head teachers, SENCOs and class teachers.

Collaboration and liaison outside the school community is time-consuming but can be highly beneficial to all concerned. Senior management will need to place a high priority on this if it is to be successful, and ensure that specific time is allocated to undertake the work involved. It is not essential for the SENCO to be responsible for all liaison work and it may be appropriate to allocate aspects of the liaison process to different members of staff, thus enhancing a whole-school awareness of the importance of the role of external agencies, other schools and parents.

Finance and budgets for SEN

The great majority of policies gave little or no information on budgets for SEN. While SENCOs interviewed expressed no particular concern over their own schools' allocation of resources to SEN, the lack of specificity concerning resource allocation in policies raises the possibility that accountability for the use of these resources will be lacking. Where that is the case, it should be remembered that it is the school governors who are ultimately responsible for the effective use of such funds. OFSTED

(1996) has shown that in the main, governors are unclear about their responsibilities in this area, and without making it specific within the policy, there is no clear means for governors to check on the use made of resources.

Similarly, the almost complete absence of reference to service level agreements with LEAs (and the funds used for these) in policies means that governors have little means of questioning the efficacy of these arrangements and the efficient use of resources here. This too is a cause for concern given the evidence of some of Bowers's (1992) respondents on the quality of peripatetic services. That research suggests that schools need support services that are responsive in terms of time and expectations and that the quality of individual personnel is important. Schools too often 'had to take what was offered rather than what they thought their schools and those they serve, the children, needed' (Bowers 1992:25). This clearly needs careful consideration in terms of what money is spent and how it is spent.

Although most SENCOs will feel confident that they are not being cheated on SEN provision by senior management teams, vigilance is nevertheless necessary in monitoring the use of budgets, especially in the light of the parallel finding by Vincent et al. (1995) that budgets are 'impenetrable and intricate'. This is especially so, if the fears of some writers that SEN funds will insidiously be lost to other areas are not to be realised.

There are also pressing concerns, revealed by recent research (Garner 1996; Lewis, Neill and Campbell 1996) into the work of the SENCO, that the main impediment to successful implementation of the Code of Practice is the lack of non-contact time given to coordinators. Greater explicitness about the use of funds may allow SENCOs to negotiate more effectively for additional time to be allotted to them to undertake their role effectively.

We would suggest, therefore, that in reviewing and developing the SEN policy the attention of the development and review team be drawn to the requirements laid out in the various circulars and regulations. In particular, we would suggest that they be reminded that the policy must:

- 'describe principles governing allocation of resources to and amongst SEN pupils' (Circular 6/94, Section 40)
- 'explain how governors ensure funds are used to help them fulfil duties under section 161(1)(a) of the 1993 Act (i.e. to make SE provision if necessary)' (Circular 6/94, Section 41)
- 'explain how governors allocate funds to ensure provision specified in statements is made' (Circular 6/94, Section 42).

Specificity is clearly important. We suggest that statements such as 'In 1995, £8342 was allocated for special needs provision and this was spent on x, y and z' are necessary. And if there are pupils with statements, '£2000 was provided by the LEA for pupils with statements and this has been used in the following way.' Transparency in how schools allocate their resources for pupils with special educational needs is essential if additional financial support for this area is to be requested of LEAs by schools.

Money for SEN provision often comes to the school from a variety of sources and the criteria by which it is allocated are not always clear. However, as stated in Circular 6/94, principles for allocation and how this is undertaken do need to be made more explicit. It may be advisable to set up transparent procedures that describe how funding comes to the school and how it is thereafter spent. This is a complex area but an important one, since it is difficult to argue for further funding if there is a lack of clarity regarding the way that the original sum has been deployed.

Conclusions

Many schools have found difficulty in addressing the task of writing a policy for SEN. The task of revising these can also present difficulties and we would suggest that the following steps may assist schools in that exercise:

- Establish a policy review and development team which includes at least one governor.
- Write clearly with an audience for the policy in mind.
- Ensure everything that should be in the policy is included; follow Circular 6/94 rather than the aide-memoir in the Code.
- Ensure that the policy is specific about spending and provides clear budget statements.
- Attempt to involve senior management and class teachers in areas of provision which will promote and foster inclusive practice in the school – the CSIE document (CSIE 1996) is useful here.
- Ensure the policy gives clear guidelines on how parents are involved, and provides information on how parents can process complaints.
- Clarify the process of collaboration with external agencies and other schools, grouping together with SENCOs from other schools, in order to share ideas.

The SEN policy is an important document for the school. It establishes the school's ethos, articulates its commitment, outlines its practice, and celebrates its successes. It can be used to develop better practice and to ensure the fair distribution of resources to learning support. With careful inclusion of other staff members, the review and monitoring of the SEN policy could serve as a strategy to enhance the status of the SENCO in school, enable a sharing of the workload and develop provision for pupils with special educational needs in the school.

Notes

1   This chapter is based upon an article entitled 'The quality of SEN policies: time for review?' in *Support for Learning* **12**(1) February 1997, 10–14.

Chapter 16

More than just managing

John Dwyfor Davies, Philip Garner and John Lee

When most teachers are asked to reflect on the changes that have taken place in education in the last 20 or 30 years, they would probably identify the 1988 Education Act as a watershed, since when the entire system has been inundated with rapid and continuous change unprecedented in any previous era. But for teachers who have substantial involvement in special education, whether in mainstream or special provision, the response to this question would almost certainly include some consideration of the impact of the Warnock Report (1978) and the subsequent Education Acts of 1981 and 1983 which implemented its proposals. Special educators, therefore, would be likely to extend the period of 'change' by at least another decade. During the 20 or so years between 1978 and the present day, therefore, those involved in SEN have responded to the legislative demands from general educators on one hand and special educators on the other. The managerial brunt of all these changes has been borne by SENCOs.

The debate surrounding policy and provision in SEN shows no sign of abating as we move towards the end of the century. At the time of writing, for example, a number of controversial policy and practice issues remain to be played out – from inclusion to professional standards for SENCOs, from levels of statementing to the burden of bureaucracy. These concerns constitute just some of those which have been identified by contributors to this book. In consequence, therefore, the indications are that the period from 1998 onwards will see further change, with an attendant pressure on SENCOs to incorporate any revisions or new initiatives into the way that special needs are currently met in schools.

Much has been made of inclusive education, particularly since the Salamanca Statement (1993) and, more parochially, the Green Paper (DfEE 1997c) – and rightly so. In absorbing the content of what continues to be a tidal wave of instruction, guidance and monitoring documentation from central government, the SENCO has to adopt a similar inclusive approach. SEN-specific material may be a high priority, but if there is to be an even remotely honest regard for the concept of inclusivity, then the SENCO needs to recognise that every official briefing or policy statement must have relevance to a population which only recently has come to be regarded as *bona-fide* members of the mainstream educational community. Whatever the subject matter and irrespective of its content, it will still form part of a dynamic agenda, for which the SENCO is the lynch-pin. Its implementation will do much to secure the conditions necessary for school improvement and effectiveness.

This summary chapter is not intended as a precis of what has gone before. To attempt this would fly in the face of one of the central themes of many of our contributors: that managing SEN in primary schools is a complex, time-consuming and frequently uncertain endeavour. Reducing it to the level of a written afterthought insults the valuable work that even Mr Woodhead has acknowledged. We have, conversely, selected a number of oppositional concepts which seem to proscribe the work that SENCOs do, and which engage them in much soul-searching and discussion. Whilst even this is not an exhaustive list, mention of just three or four gives some idea of the dilemmas currently facing SENCOs.

Amongst the implications we identify the following:

- management and leadership;
- arbitration and advocacy;
- entitlement and surveillance;
- bureaucratic maximism and minimalism.

The rest of this chapter will explore these issues within a grounded framework under the themes of *policy*, *roles* and *procedures*, which could be said to comprise the structural components of the Code of Practice (Garner 1995). Their complexities and significance for the function of the SENCO prompt us to suggest that the SENCO is not simply a manager, with its implications of 'implementing other people's decisions'. What we are trying to convey, in the spirit of the contributions to this book, is that to be a successful SENCO, measured in terms of outcomes for the children, means the ability to rationalise and balance what may, at first sight, appear to be contradictory concepts.

Policy

In our introduction to this chapter, we have pointed to the way in which, for over 20 years, those involved in SEN have been the object of policy-makers' gaze. Legislation and administrative instruments which, rhetorically speaking, appear child-centred and enabling, have also provided the means for centralised surveillance and regulation. The paradox inherent in this situation is not for the faint-hearted. To be effective, the occasion now seems to demand that SENCOs do not get locked into a mechanistic cycle but, rather, take on the function of a local change agent. In other words, they need to exercise leadership rather than management. While SENCOs are bound by legislation and administrative orders, to comply with, for example, the Code, they are not without power in the way that this is interpreted at local level. Each SENCO needs to establish a personal agenda regarding critical reflection of how they make things happen within their own school. Kathy Bale gives a good example of this in her chapter where she describes how the SENCO becomes instrumental in adapting elements of the Code: for example, a decision to formalise Stage 1 procedures in her school was taken because of the perception of need at local level. In another chapter, Sheila Russell has also provided a very practical example, in which she reallocates the resources provided by the Local Education Authority in a way deemed to be more effective and advantageous to the pupil than that initially intended by the resource giver – again a case of leadership over managerialism in policy matters.

OFSTED inspections require substantial documentation regarding provision for children with learning difficulties. The SENCO is integrally involved in the production of this monitoring material. In one sense, therefore, she functions as an agent of surveillance on the part of central government – whilst also being the subject of scrutiny herself. A simple preoccupation with management will lead to the SENCO operating as an enforcer, rather than an enabler. As an illustration of this concept, we can consider evidence of the operation of OFSTED inspectors themselves who apply personal judgement and reinterpret inspection documentation in order to benefit the school under inspection. Lee and Fitz (1997) cite interviews with registered inspectors who question the validity of the term 'serious weaknesses' and therefore judge schools to be 'satisfactory' or 'in need of special measures'. By analogy, SENCOs have the capacity to use and interpret the Code's overall policy thrust, as they can with other audit requirements, to advantage, rather than as big-brother agenda.

As we note in the first chapter of this book, current policy is underpinned by the school effectiveness movement. It is likely that the present preoccupation with measurable outcomes and targets delivered by a prescribed pedagogy within a (usually) hourly time frame (Literacy and Numeracy 'Hours' are cases in point) will remain in place in the foreseeable future. For special educational needs, the IEP retains an almost totemic importance, and remains the topic which most SENCOs find themselves drawn to whenever cluster meetings or other collaborative gatherings take place. But as we have noted in various points in this book, the IEP's relationship to what is undertaken in, for example, the Literacy Hour, will be the subject of increasing scrutiny (OFSTED 1997). Many of the early attempts to provide IEP formats in the period following the publication of the Code in 1994 ended in epics of Tolstoyan proportions, accompanied by complaints that they were unworkable in practice and added a burdensome bureaucratic device to an already immense workload. Moreover, there was not necessarily a demonstrable link between what was written in the IEP and what actually happened in the classroom, as OFSTED inspectors were quick to point out. In a word, it was the kind of situation which gets bureaucracy a bad name.

If we take an optimistic view of the 'Two Hours', as they are now euphemistically titled, and regard their content and pedagogy as being highly focused and differentiated, it should consequently be possible to write slimmer and more pertinent IEPs. This change in planning procedure could be liberating for the SENCO enabling her to spend less time on paperwork and more time advising and supporting colleagues in the delivery of the curriculum. Here again, we are indicating a move away from management towards leadership. Freedom from the constraints of the word-processor might also mean more real time teaching children.

Roles

Given the challenges facing special education as a whole (and inclusive education in particular), the SENCO has to consider carefully her role. Is she an arbitrator or an advocate? If she perceives her role as one of advocacy, on whose behalf does she act? Her position may be somewhat analogous to that of the education psychologist whose role has traditionally been regarded with a degree of circumspection. EPs are the principal gate-keepers of provision for children with SEN, and yet that provision is a finite resource delivered by their employer. In much the same way, the SENCO has become the arbiter of a predetermined level of resourcing within her school. Does this compromise her role as advocate on behalf of children with learning difficulty? For both EPs and SENCOs the level of resourcing is beyond their control; but this does not preclude them from arguing for, and gaining, extra resource for their school, or individual pupils, from a limited budget.

Acknowledgement also has to be made that the operational instruments of the Code act in a dual capacity which can sometimes assume the level of perversity. On the one hand, the level of bureaucracy may inhibit the action of SENCOs as decision makers over resources. On the other hand, its guidelines provide the statutory equipment to enable the SENCO to promote ends defined by the needs of pupils and schools. In other words, when the going gets tough the SENCO can resort to statutory instruments to influence others – this is one of the major positive effects of the Code. Whilst none of us would argue for the use of the Code as a nuclear deterrent, it nevertheless makes a good conventional missile.

Balancing these two role orientations presents the SENCO with a major challenge. The rapid onset of procedural requirements over the last 20 years has possibly had a hitherto unacknowledged effect on the way that special needs teachers now relate to children with learning difficulties. Each of the authors recalls a period when heads of remedial departments operated according to a personalised, as opposed to an institutionalised, way. In the 1960s and early 1970s for example, it was common for heads of remedial departments to focus almost exclusively on their perception of what comprised the child's learning needs. In doing this, the pupil's entitlement to a broad and balanced curriculum played little part. Nevertheless, their actions were rooted in practice rather than ideology and were personalised to individual cases.

There is a danger that more recent practices are dependent on an institutionalised approach. Here, although on the face of it there is a more inclusive philosophy, it is important to question whether what happens to the individual child has the same importance for decision making now. In the past, remedial teachers prioritised the impact of provision rather than the procedures that delineated it. In many cases, what was deemed to be needed was not appropriate and often when it was, it was provided in a restricted and formulaic manner. Maintaining the safeguards of procedure, whilst at the same time ensuring a proper address to individual needs, remains a core function of the SENCO's role. This often places them in a contradictory position between the perception of individual needs (inadequacies) and entitlement to the school experience.

Procedures

Since its inception, those responsible for special needs provision in schools have maintained that the Code of Practice has placed a significant burden on them. In the case we are here discussing, i.e. primary school teachers, this is in addition to a range of other statutory requirements and their traditional functions as a class teacher. The level of duress imposed by this may have seriously inhibited the honourable intentions of the Code writers. The Code was constructed as 'guidance' but seems to have been understood as prescription. If the Code is to be made more relevant to what goes on in schools (in other words, the fact that its guidelines are actually implemented), some rationalisation and prioritisation of its content needs to take place. SENCOs need to revisit the concept of 'guidance' and be confident in interpreting the good practice it describes so that they meet the needs of their own circumstances.

One way of securing the impact of the Code across every level of the school, from pupil through parent, class teacher to senior manager, is to adopt a Dearing approach to its content. SENCOs need to think about what has made the most impact on the learning difficulties of children over the last four years. Such procedures as whole-school approaches, EPs, differentiation, collaborative teaching and learning, home–school links and so on might figure in a prioritised list. How are these procedures supported by documentation? How accessible to all is the documentation? Furthermore, and critically, how essential is it that it exists in written form? Finally, if it is regarded as fundamental, how long should it be? Consideration of factors such as these need to be viewed in the context of the cautionary points raised by Bill Evans earlier in this volume.

Effective collaboration with others has been one of the salient features of good practice in SEN, and has been central to policy making since Warnock. The SENCO is fulcrum to much of this activity, coordinating discussion and decision making between other teachers, classroom assistants, parents. the pupils themselves and significant professionals from outside the school. The official emphasis placed on this kind of activity is not matched by the opportunities provided for the SENCO to perform the task, as most studies on the views of SENCOs have substantiated and as has been exemplified by some of our contributors. Indeed, one may be forgiven for suggesting that this is perhaps the most glaring example of the discrepancy between rhetoric and reality in the Code, a situation which prompts understandable cynicism from many SENCOs.

Here again, however, the SENCO can act proactively. One way of working is to accept the concept of marketisation at face value. In much the same way that the LEAs now construct their SEN support activity in the form of a 'business unit', so too can the SENCO operate in a manner in which she allocates finite portions of time according to needs. Several SENCOs we have spoken to during the course of producing this book have commented that there is a tendency for them to be 'sucked in' to a small group of children with learning difficulties (and particular teachers...) with the net result being that they are unable to offer service elsewhere in the school. It is, therefore, vital that the SENCO, in collaboration with her senior management team, define more explicitly the way in which she will organise her time. This has to be transparent, with all colleagues in the school being made aware of the likely levels of direct involvement that they can expect from the SENCO.

Whose Code is it anyway?

There appears to be a perception among some teachers that the Code of Practice is an onerous procedure, there only to make their life difficult. Viewed in this way, the Code is the property of the central bureaucracy and is simply another aspect of regulation and control. If this is the case, then the situation is bleak indeed. It has become very fashionable to talk in terms of policy ownership as one component of social justice. If by ownership is meant direct involvement in the writing of policy, then the Code of Practice can only be owned by a small bureaucratic elite and the process of consultation, like that of the SENCOs themselves, is simply a rhetorical loop. Furthermore, a by-product of imposition is disempowerment through lack of ownership. Much of the tenor of the Code as it was written in 1994 was to be viewed as a dynamic, working document for the use of teachers and the benefit of children, amended to suit particular contexts.

SENCOs could take an idealistic child-centred view of the Code. This will inevitably lead them into conflicts about resources and, perhaps more significantly, the actual placement of children. It follows that engagement with such things will also lead into debates with colleagues and other professionals which may highlight highly polarised stances. If it is decided that the Code belongs to the parents/guardians and the child, similar conflicts are likely to arise. It may also leave the SENCO in the position of operating as an advocate, not for the child alone, but for the parents' perception of the child's needs.

The Code of Practice should be viewed more in terms of being a charter for the enhancement of individual needs, based upon minimalist prescription of how significant adults in the process collaborate with each other to secure this goal. In putting this principle into practice it is not helpful to ignore the institutional and organisational context of the Code because it is only within these frameworks that it can be operated. Thus, whilst SENCOs need to continue to develop their capacity to share one another's experiences and evidence of good practice, they also need to ensure that the particularised contexts of their own schools are kept in sharp focus.

Irrespective of the current mode of deference to the pronouncements of quangos, PANDA droppings and miscellaneous snakes in the grass, the SENCO, as the contributions in this volume demonstrate, is – and will continue to be – pivotal to future developments. What will become apparent, too, is that their managerial influences will begin to expand beyond the confines of SEN as it has been traditionally constructed, as the impact of inclusive practice gathers force.

Bibliography

Advisory Centre for Education (1994) 'Preparing for the Code of Practice: issues for governors', *ACF Bulletin* **58**, 9–12.

Ainscow, M. (1991) 'Effective schools for all: an alternative approach to special needs in education', in Ainscow, M. (ed.) *Effective Schools for All*. London: David Fulton Publishers.

Athey, C. (1990) *Extending Thought in Young Children – A Parent Teacher Partnership*. London: Chapman Publishing Ltd.

Audit Commission/HMI (1992) *Getting the Act Together: Provision for Pupils with Special Needs: A Management Handbook for Schools and LEAs*. London: HMSO.

Audit Commission (1994) *The Act Moves On: Progress in Special Educational Needs*. London: HMSO.

Audit Commission (1998) *Changing Partners: a Discussion on the Role of the Local Education Authority*. London: HMSO.

Ballard, K. (1995) 'Inclusion, paradigms, power and participation', in Clark, C., Dyson, A., Millward, A. (eds) *Towards Inclusive Schools?* London: David Fulton Publishers.

Bartholomew, L. and Bruce, T. (1993) *Getting to Know*. London: Hodder & Stoughton.

Bines, H. (1986) *Redefining Remedial Education*. London: Croom Helm.

Bines, H. (1995) 'Special educational needs in the market place', *Journal of Education Policy* **10**(2), 157–171.

Bines, H. and Loxley, A. (1996) 'Implementing the Code of Practice', *Oxford Review of Education*
21, 381–394.

Bines, H. and Thomas, G. (1994) 'From bureaucrats to advocates? The changing role of local education authorities', *Support for Learning* **9**(2), 61–67.

Blunkett, D. (1997) Speech 13 May, DfEE.

Bowe, R. and Ball, S. J., with Gold, A. (1992) *Reforming Education and Changing Schools*. London: Routledge.

Bowers, T. (1992) 'A question of support', *Special Children* **54**, 23–5.

Bruce, T. (1991) *Time to Play in Early Childhood Education*. London: Hodder & Stoughton

Bruce, T. (1994) 'Play, the universe and everything', in Moyle, J. R. (ed.), *The Excellence of Play*, 189–98. Buckingham: Open University Press.

Bruce, T. (1997) *Early Childhood Education*. London: Hodder & Stoughton.

Bruce, T., Findley, A., Read, J. and Scarborough, M. (1995) *Recurring Themes in Education*. London: Paul Chapman Publishing Ltd.

Bruner, J. (1985) 'Vygotsky: a historical and conceptual perspective', in Wertsch, J. V. (ed.) (1985), *Culture, Communication and Cognition*, 21–34. Cambridge: Cambridge University Press.

Bruner, J. (1986) *Actual Minds, Possible Worlds*. Cambridge, Massachusetts and London: Harvard University Press.

Butterworth, S. and Light, P. (eds) (1982) *Social Cognition in Studies of the Development of Understanding*. Brighton: Harvester.

Byers, S. (1998) Speeches to North of England Education Conference, Bradford, 7 January and 4 October.

Clark, C., Dyson, A., Skidmore, D., Millward, A. (1997) *New Directions in Special Needs*. London: Cassell.

Clough, P. and Barton, L. (eds) (1995) *Making Difficulties: Research and the Construction of Special Educational Needs*. London: Paul Chapman Publishing Ltd.

Croll, P. and Moses, D. (1985) *One in Five*, London: Routledge.

Croll, P. and Moses, D. (1998) 'Pragmatism, ideology and educational change: the case of special educational needs', *British Journal of Educational Studies* **46**(1) 11–25.

CSIE (Council for Studies on Inclusive Education) (1996) *Developing an Inclusive Policy for Your School*. Bristol: CSIE.

Curry, M. and Bloomfield, C. (1995) *Personal and Social Education for Primary Schools Through Circle Time*. Tamworth: NASEN Enterprise Ltd.

Davie, R. (1996) 'Raising the achievements of pupils with special educational needs', *Support for Learning* **11**(2), 51–56.

Deem, T., Brehony, K., Heath, S. (1995) *Active Citizenship and the Governing of Schools*. Buckingham: Open University Press.

Department for Education and Science (1978) *Special Educational Needs (The Warnock Report)*. London: HMSO.

Department for Education (1993) *Education for Disaffected Pupils*. HMSO.

Department for Education (1994) *Code of Practice on Identification and Assessment of Special Educational Needs*. London: DfE.

Department for Education and Employment (1997a) *School Governors: A Guide to the Law*. London: HMSO.

Department for Education and Employment (1997b) *The SENCO Guide*. London: HMSO.

Department for Education and Employment (1997c) *Excellence for All Children: Meeting Special Educational Needs*. London: HMSO.

Department for Education and Employment (1997d) *Excellence in Schools*. London: DfEE.

Department for Education and Employment (1998a) *National Literacy Strategy Framework for Teaching*. London: DfEE.

Department for Education and Employment (1998b) *National Numeracy Strategy*. London: DfEE.

Derrington, C., Evants, C., Lee, B. (1996) *The Code in Practice: The Impact on Schools and LEAs*. Slough: NFER

Dessent, T. (1987) *Making the Ordinary School Special*. Lewes: Falmer Press.

Drummond, M. J. (1993) *Assessing Children's Learning*. London: David Fulton Publishers.

Duffy, M. (n.d.) *A Better System of Inspection*. Hexham: OFSTIN.

Dyer, C. (1995) 'The Code of Practice through LEA eyes' *British Journal of Special Education* **22**(2), 48–51.

Dyson, A. (1990) 'Effective learning consultancy: a future role for special needs coordinators?', *Support for Learning* **5**(3), 116–127.

Dyson, A. (1991) 'Rethinking roles, redefining concepts: special needs teachers in mainstream schools', *Support for Learning* **6**(2), 51–60.

Dyson, A. and Gains, C. (1995) 'The Role of the Special Needs Coordinator: poisoned chalice or crock of gold?' *Support for Learning* **10**(2), 50–56.

Edwards, A. (1998) 'Educational psychology: partnership: in the development of theory and practice' *Psychology of Education Review*. **22**(1).

Evans, R., Docking, J., Berkely, D., Evans, C. (1995) *Review of Policies in Five Local Authorities*. London: Roehampton Institute.

Fitz, J. and Lee, J. (1996) 'Where angels fear' in Ouston, J., Early, P., Fidler, B. (eds) *OFSTED Inspections: The Early Experience*. London: David Fulton Publishers.

Galligan, D. J. (1986) *Discretionary Powers: a Legal Study of Official Discretion*. Oxford: Clarendon Press.

Ganz, G.(1987) *Quasi-legislation: Recent Developments in Secondary Legislation*. London: Sweet & Maxwell.

Garner, P. (1995) 'Sense or nonsense? Dilemmas in the SEN Code of Practice', *Support for Learning* **10**(1), 3–7.

Garner, P. (1996) 'Go forth and coordinate! What Special Needs Coordinators think about the Code of Practice', *School Organisation* **16**(2), 155–64.

Garner, P., Hinchcliffe, V, Sandow, S. (1995) *What Teachers Do*. London: Paul Chapman Publishing Ltd.

Garner, P. and Sandow, S. (eds) (1995) *Advocacy, Self-Advocacy and Special Educational Needs*. London: David Fulton Publishers.

Gurney, P. (1988) *Self Esteem in Children with Special Educational Needs*. London: Routledge.

Hardwick, J. (1998) 'Just Typical'. *Special Children* (March), 12–15.

Hart, S. (1991) 'Differentiation – ways forward or retreat', *British Journal of Special Education* **19**(1), 10–12.

Hart, S. (1996) *Differentiation and the Secondary Curriculum*. London: Routledge.

Haviland, J. (1988) *Take Care Mr Baker*. London: Fourth Estate.

Hopkins, D. and Harris, A. (1997) 'Improving the quality of education for all', *Support for Learning* **12**(4), 147–151.

Hurst, V. (1994) 'Observing play in early childhood', in Moyle, J. R. (ed.), *The Excellence of Play*, 173–88. Buckingham: Open University Press.

Jeffrey, B. and Woods, P. (1996) 'Feeling deprofessionalised: the social construction of emotions during OFSTED inspection'. *Cambridge Journal of Education* **26**(3), 325–344.

Lee, J. and Fiz, J. (1997) 'HMI and OFSTED: evolution or revolution in school inspection', *Journal of Educational Studies* **45**(1), 22–52.

Lewin, K. (1935) *A Dynamic Theory of Personality. Selected Papers*. New York and London: McGraw Hill.

Lewis, A. (1995) *Special Needs Provision in Mainstream Primary Schools*. Stoke-on-Trent: Trentham.

Lewis, A., Neill, S. R., St J., Campbell, R. J. (1996) *The Implementation of the Code of Practice in Primary and Secondary Schools: A National Survey of Perceptions of Special Educational Needs Coordinators*. London: NUT.

Lloyd, S. and Berthelot, C. (1992) *Self Empowerment: How to Get What You Want From Life*. London: Kogan Page.

Lunt, I., Evans, J., Norwich, B., Wedell, K. (1994) *Working Together: Inter-School Collaboration for Special Needs*. London: Cassell.

MacNamara, S. and Moreton, G. (1997) *Understanding Differentiation*. London: David Fulton Publishers.

Maslow, A. (1943) 'A theory of human motivation', *Psychology Review* **50**, 370–96.

Mortimore, P., Sammons, P., Stoll, L., Lewis, D. and Ecob, R. (1988) *School Matters: The Junior Years*. Wells: Open Books.

Moyle, J. R. (ed.) (1994) *The Excellence of Play*. Buckingham: Open University Press.

Nash, R. (1973) *Classrooms Observed. The Teacher's Perception and the Pupil's Performance*. London: Routledge and Kegan Paul Ltd.

National Curriculum Council (1989) *A Curriculum for All*. York: NCC.

National Literacy Project (1997) *Draft Framework for Teachers* (March). The National Project for Literacy and Numeracy, National Centre, London House, 59–65 London Road, Berkshire.

Newton, C., Taylor, G. and Wilson, D. (1996) 'Circles of Friends: an inclusive approach to meeting emotional and behavioural needs', *Educational Psychology in Practice* **12**(1).

Nicholls, R. (ed.) (1986) *Rumpus Schema Extra*. Cleveland: Teachers in Early Education.

OFSTED (1995a) *Guidance on the Inspection of Nursery and Primary Schools*. London: HMSO.

OFSTED (1995b) *Guidance on the Inspection of Secondary Schools*. London: HMSO.

OFSTED (1995c) *Guidance on the Inspection of Special Schools*. London: HMSO.

OFSTED (1996) *The Implementation of the Code of Practice.* London: OFSTED.

OFSTED (1997) *The SEN Code of Practice: Two Years On.* London: OFSTED.

OFSTED (1998a) *The Annual Report of Her Majesty's Chief Inspector of Schools, 1996-97.* London: OSTED.

OFSTED (1998b) *School Evaluation Matters.* London: HMSO.

Reynolds, D. (1991) 'Changing ineffective schools' in Ainscow, M. (ed.) *Effective Schools for All.* London: David Fulton Publishers.

Rice, S. (1996) An Investigation of Schemas as a way of Supporting and Extending Young Children's Learning. Bristol: UWE (unpublished M.Ed thesis).

Roaf, C. and Bines, H. (1988) 'Needs, rights and opportunities in special education', in Roaf, C. and Bines, H. (eds) *Needs, Rights and Opportunities: Developing Approaches to Special Education*, 20–27. Lewes: The Falmer Press.

Roberts, R. (1995) *Self-Esteem and Successful Learning.* London: Hodder & Stoughton.

Schools Curriculum and Assessment Authority (1997) *Baseline Assessment.* London: SCAA.

Scott, L. (1993) *Governors and Special Education: Report of the Enquiry Into Governor Training for SEN.* London: Advisory Centre for Education.

Scott-Baumann, A. (1996) 'Listen to the child' in Jones, K. and Charlton, T. (eds) *Overcoming Learning and Behaviour Difficulties.* London: Routledge.

Scott-Baumann, A., Bloomfield, A., Roughton, L. (1997) *Becoming a Secondary School Teacher.* London: Hodder and Stroughton.

Sebba, J. and Ainscow, M. (1996) 'International developments in inclusive schooling: mapping the issues', *Cambridge Journal of Education* **26**(1), 5–17.

SENTC (1996) *Professional Development to Meet Special Educational Needs: Report to the DfEE.* Stafford: SENTC.

SENTC (1996). *Professional Development to Meet Special Educational Needs.* Stafford: SENTC.

Slavin, R. (1997) *Success for All: Policy Implications for British Education.* Speech to Literacy Task Force Consultative Conference, 27 February.

Stafford, S. (1998) 'Chronic fatigue syndrome: seeing the real ME', *Special!* (Spring), 6–9.

Stakes, R. and Hornby, G. (1997) *Change in Special Education.* London: Cassell.

Teacher Training Agency (1997) *Consultation Paper on National Standards for Special Educational Needs Coordinators.* London: TTA.

Teacher Training Agency (1998) *National Standards for Special Educational Needs Coordinators.* London: TTA.

Thomas, G. and Tarr, J. (1996) *The Monitoring and Evaluation of Schools' SEN Policies.* Bristol: University of the West of England.

Tod, J., Blamires, M. (1998) 'IEPs – speech and language', in Tod, J., Castle, F., Blamires, M., *IEPs: Implementing Effective Practice.* London: David Fulton Publishers.

Tod, J., Castle, F. and Blamires, M. (1998) *IEPs: Implementing Effective Practice.* London: David Fulton Publishers.

University of Warwick (1996) *The Implementation of the Code of Practice in Primary and Secondary Schools: A National Survey of Perceptions of Special Educational Needs Coordinators*. Coventry: University of Warwick Institute of Education.

Vincent, C., Evans, J., Lunt, I, Young, P. (1994) 'The market forces? The effect of local management of schools on special educational needs provision', *British Educational Research Journal* **20**(3), 261–77.

Vincent, C., Evans, J., Lunt, I., Young, P. (1995) 'Policy and practice: the changing nature of special educational provision in schools', *British Journal of Special Education* **22**(1), 4–11.

Welton, J. (1988) 'Incrementalism to catastrophe theory: policy for children with special educational needs', in Roaf, C. and Bines, H. (eds) *Needs, Rights and Opportunities: Developing Approaches to Special Education*, 5–19. Lewes: The Falmer Press.

Whalley, M. (1997) *Working with Parents*. London: Hodder & Stoughton.

Index